One Potato
Two Potato

By Anne Cotton and Fran Martin

Illustrated by Lyn Hope

D1465894

Published by
Teaching Resource Center
P.O. Box 1509
San Leandro, CA 94577

Printed in the United States of America
ISBN: 1–56785–015–4

Contents

Blacklines

The Basic Teaching Strategies

In the development of this theme you will find such phrases as **brainstorm for, develop in the pocket chart, sort and classify**, etc. To help clarify these phrases we have listed these basic teaching strategies and have given a brief description of each.

Fill with language:

This is when we read to the children. We read not only stories but poetry and factual information as well. We begin with a discussion of the illustrations to develop as much oral language as possible. We stop periodically to provide the opportunity for the child to anticipate and predict what might happen next. We also read a selection many times over to help make that selection become a part of the child. We feel strongly that we must continually *fill the child with language* as we move ahead with the theme.

Chanting:

Children need to work orally with the patterns of language. The primary way to do this with very young children is by chanting. This technique helps instill the rhythm and structure of language which then becomes a part of their everyday speech.

One way to chant is by using the my turn, your turn technique. The teacher reads a phrase and the children echo this phrase. The teacher tracks (runs hand under the text, pointing to each word) as the chanting takes place. Children may chant using the whole text (pictures, pictures and words, or words alone), or merely chant a repetitive phrase ("Not I," said the dog.) Chanting may be done using big books, charts, brainstorming ideas, pocket chart activities, trade books, etc. Songs and poems should also be included. When working with songs and poetry, we often add rhythmic hand movements which help instill the rhythm of the language and enhances the memorization.

Brainstorming:

Brainstorming is when children orally respond to a question posed by the teacher with the results usually being recorded where they may be seen by the children. This gives the teacher an insight into the children's knowledge. We usually begin a theme by brainstorming for what the children know about a given subject. A lack of ideas indicates that the children may need a *refill* of language and knowledge. The brainstorming is continuously being added to as the theme is developed.

Brainstorming is a whole class activity. The teacher begins by asking a question such as "What is green?" and elicits responses from the children. As the children respond, the teacher draws the appropriate pictures on the chalkboard and the children chant. **Note:** at the beginning of the kindergarten year, draw a picture only. No words are needed.

After the brainstorming, again chant all the pictures that were drawn: "A leaf is green. A turtle is green. Grass is green. A car is green." As the year progresses you will want to add words to the brainstorming:

Most brainstorming needs to be saved! As you work through a theme you will be continually referring to these ideas. Copy the brainstorming onto cards or chart paper. The cards may be displayed using masking tape, sticky side out. The chart may be used for matching and rebuilding. At a later date the chart may be cut apart and made into a strip book.

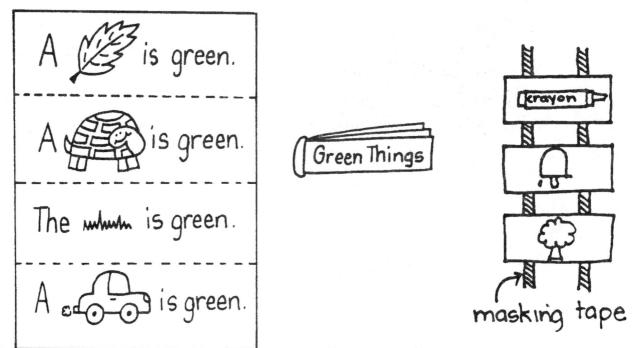

Another example of a brainstorming technique is to record ideas in categories that are not labeled. After the pattern is obvious, the children tell where to record the next idea. This method helps stimulate the children's thinking.

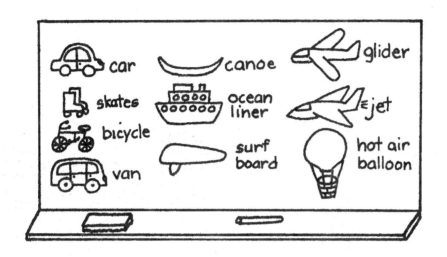

Sorting and Classifying:

This when children look for likenesses and differences and put things together that are alike in some manner. The ideas from brainstorming activities are ideal for sorting and classifying. We usually begin classifying with groups of four to six children, with each group having about twenty cards or items to sort.

After this small group sorting activity, the whole class regroups and chants. Example: We classified according to color and then chanted, "A chair is green. An olive is green. A fat frog is green, etc." Gradually, we work toward activities that will involve individual classifications. The results of these activities may be graphed, producing either a real graph or a pictorial graph.[1]

Develop in the Pocket Chart:

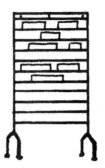

We use a pocket chart made of clear acetate and nylon.[2] You may use sentence strips or tagboard cards (laminated or contacted for a longer life) with the pocket chart. Whole texts, repeated phrases or pictures only may be used. There are a variety of ways to use the pocket chart. We listed our favorites:

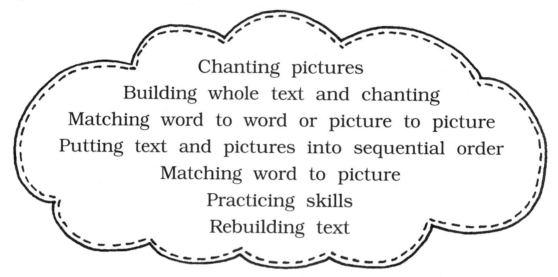

Chanting pictures
Building whole text and chanting
Matching word to word or picture to picture
Putting text and pictures into sequential order
Matching word to picture
Practicing skills
Rebuilding text

When we are developing a lesson in the pocket chart, we usually insert the appropriate pictures, or text and pictures, and then have the children chant **many** times. We may ask the children to hide their eyes and then we take something out of the text or merely turn it over.

The children then decide what is missing and chant to see if they are correct. We then take more than one word, picture, or phrase out (or turn them over) and repeat the process. The final task is to rebuild the entire text.

Samples:

Step 1:   Chanting pictures
"A leaf is green."

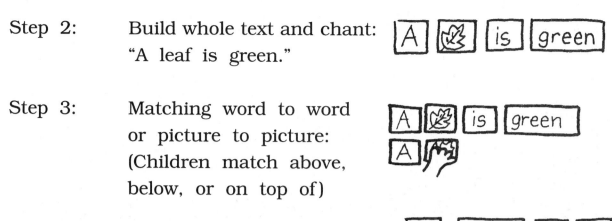

Step 2: Build whole text and chant:
"A leaf is green."

Step 3: Matching word to word
or picture to picture:
(Children match above,
below, or on top of)

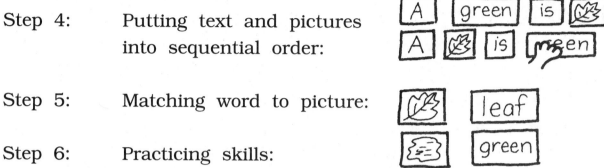

Step 4: Putting text and pictures
into sequential order:

Step 5: Matching word to picture:

Step 6: Practicing skills:

- Find the word that says *green*.
- Find the word that says *is*.
- Find the word that comes before *green*.
- Find the word that comes after *is*.
- What sound do you hear at the
beginning of the word *leaf*?

Step 7: Rebuilding: All pictures and text are distributed to
the children and the complete story is built again in
the pocket chart. Children read the text from the pocket
chart, checking for accuracy.

Tracking:

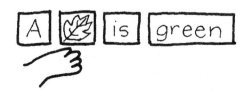

This involves moving your hand under
and pointing to each word as it is read.
This helps develop left to right pro-

gression as well as one-to-one correspondence between the printed text and the spoken word.

Big Books:

These are enlarged versions of books, poems or songs. The print must be large enough so that it may be seen by the entire class. The enlarged print allows us to track as we read and helps to develop one-to-one correspondence. Many of the activities used with the pocket chart may also be used with big books. We laminate the pages of teacher-prepared big books and bind them with loose leaf rings. The rings may be taken out and the pages shuffled so that the children may sequence the big book. For obvious reasons **do not** number the pages. These books are really loved and used over and over by the children.

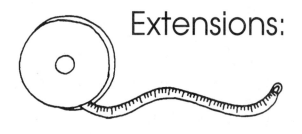

Extensions:

These are activities we practice what we learned during brainstorming, reading, chanting, and the various pocket chart activities. We try to incorporate the following:

Individual booklets – Each child makes his/her own booklet and should have the opportunity to read and track before taking it home.

Class book – Each child contributes a page and the book is kept in the classroom library.

Drama – Children act out the activity with **all** children taking **all** the parts. (a bit noisy but very effective)

Art – Children make illustrations for bulletin boards, booklets, plays, etc., using as many different kinds of art media as possible.

Make-a-play – Children retell a story by manipulating characters they have made.

Writing – All writing activities need to be extensively developed orally **first.**

1. Using a structure or frame, the children fill in the blanks by taking the ideas from the brainstorming activities.

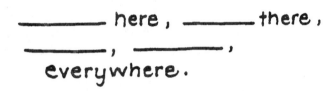

2. Creating innovations: children orally rewrite a familiar text using their own words. Example: (change "Brown bear, brown bear, what do you see?" to "Octopus, Octopus, what do you see?") This can be an individual or a whole group activity. The teacher may need to take dictation for the very young child.

3. Dictation: children individually illustrate and the teacher transcribes for them.

Draw with me – This is a whole class activity where language development is the goal. We do not consider this an art lesson. All the children are working with individual chalkboards at this time. We ask the children to name all the parts that need to be included to draw a specific object. A sample follows on the next page.

"What do we need to make a house?"

"A door"

"A roof"

"Windows"

(continue until entire picture is completed)

Individual sequencing – This is when each child puts pictures or a text into a specific order. This is usually a *cut and paste* activity. It varies in difficulty. We begin with pictures only, then pictures with the text, and finally the text alone. We also put the text in sequence with numerals, words, and pictures.

Pictures only:

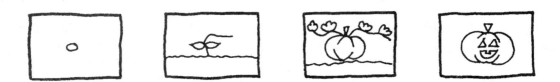

Pictures with text:

Numeral, text and picture:

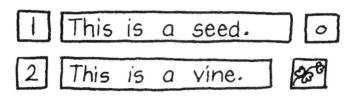

Homework – This is when we try to involve the family. The homework is occasional and we include a detailed explanation. This activity is returned to class and used for chanting, classifying booklet making or other language activities.

An example might be:

Dear Parents,

Our language arts theme this month is centered around plants. This week we are learning about seeds. Your child needs to bring a picture of something that grows from a seed. You may help your child draw or find a picture in a magazine. Please return the picture tomorrow.

Thank you for helping!

A follow-up activity might include sorting and classifying these pictures according to whether the plant produces food or not, i.e., flower, grapes, oak tree, oranges, etc. A booklet can then be made including all the homework pictures or individual booklets may be made from each classification.

- -

1. Baratta-Lorton, Mary. *Mathematics Their Way*, Addison-Wesley Publishing Company, Reading, MA 1976.
2. Available from **Teaching Resource Center**, P.O. Box 1509, 14023 Catalina Street, San Leandro, CA 94577.

Introduction

Welcome to our thematic learning feast! Try not to think about calories as you eat your way through *One Potato, Two Potato.* Very few things can capture the attention of a young child more completely than food, glorious food!

We found it very difficult to narrow down our enormous stack of literature for this theme. Obtaining the materials is quite easy and fun! The difficulty lies in making choices so that we include a variety of teaching strategies. There is a great deal of excellent literature – in fact it is conceivable to teach a food theme for months. The tightness of our clothing dictated it was time to bring this theme to an end.

If you wish to use the big books we have referred to in the text, we suggest you send for them 3 – 4 weeks before you wish to begin this theme, as it takes a while for the books to arrive and you will need time to prepare them. The addresses are as follows:

Ten Crunchy Carrots
Whole Language Resources
P.O. Box 426
Hilmar, CA 95324
Phone (209) 668-4142

On Top Of Spaghetti
The Big Book Bin, Inc.
2570 Cyril Street
P.O. Box 8000
Abbotsford, B.C. V2S 6H1

This theme is written in a specific sequence, but it is merely a suggestion. You need not follow this exact order. Choose those activities that best suit your classroom. We are sure that you have many favorites of your own that you will want to add.

At the time this book went to press all the books we have developed were in print. However, books are going in and out of print all the time. If you cannot locate a particular selection, try the public library, your school library, or a second-hand bookstore. Sometimes a local bookstore will have information as to where an out of print book may be found.

Bon Appetit

Theme At A Glance

Trade Books & Big Books

Bread, Bread, Bread
Eating the Alphabet
Eggs for Tea
Growing Vegetable Soup
Let's Eat
More Spaghetti I Say
Pot Luck
Stone Soup
The Biggest Sandwich Ever
The Doorbell Rang
This Is the Bear and the Picnic
    Lunch
Today Is Monday

Aikendrum
I Like Hot Dogs
Munch, Munch, Munch
On Top of Spaghetti
Ten Crunchy Carrots

Class Books & Booklets

An Alphabet Book with Food
Going On A Picnic (children's illustrations)
Going On A Picnic (photographs)
I Like (re-write)
Jelly In A Bowl
See the Garden Grow
Stone Soup
We Don't Like

Tasting Time
Today Is Monday
Yum!

Songs

Aikendrum
Going On A Picnic
I Like Hot Dogs
I'm A Little Teapot
Munch, Munch, Munch
On Top of Spaghetti

See the Garden Grow
Ten Crunchy Carrots
Today Is Monday

Art

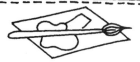

Aikendrum illustration
Going On A Picnic mural
Vegetable prints
Today Is Monday bulletin board
Today Is Monday booklet pages
   - tissue art
    - sponge painting

Science & Math

Graphing - breads, potatoes, pasta & sauce, vegetables
Planting vegetables
Sink & Float - fruits & vegetables
Sorting & Classifying

Subtraction or Addition Equations (re-writes)
Eggs for Tea
Ten Crunchy Carrots
The Doorbell Rang

Drama

Eggs for Tea
Pease Porridge Hot
Polly Put the Kettle On
Stone Soup
Teddy Bear's Picnic

Ten Crunchy Carrots
The Doorbell Rang

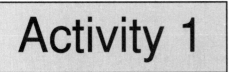

I Like Hot Dogs

Materials:

Materials needed:

- *Let's Eat,* by True Kelley
- Blacklines 1–18 for a big book
- Blacklines 19–23 for the pocket chart
- Twenty pieces of 5″ x 6″ tagboard cards for mounting the pocket chart pictures
- Blacklines 24–34 for a food wordbank
- Sixty-two pieces of 4″ x 5″ tagboard cards for mounting the food pictures
- Sentence strips
- Thirteen pieces of 12″ x 18″ black or dark blue construction paper for the big book
- Collection of food pictures for the pocket chart
- Butcher paper
- Felt pens
- Laminating film or contact paper
- Three loose leaf rings

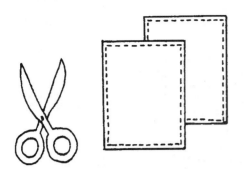

Preparation:

1. Color, cut and mount the pocket chart pictures from blacklines 19–23 on 5″ x 6″ tagboard cards. Contact or laminate.

2. Text is as follows:

> **I like hot dogs.**
> **I like beans.**
> **I like eating in my jeans.**
>
> **I like french fries.**
> **I like yams.**
> **I like eating in my jams.**
>
> **I like cookies.**
> **I like pie.**
> **I like eating in my tie.**
>
> **I like bagels.**
> **I like lox.**
> **I like eating in my socks.**
>
> **I like pancakes.**
> **I like molasses.**
> **I like eating in my glasses.**
>
> **I like veggies.**
> **I like fruits.**
> **I like eating in my boots.**

3. For the pocket chart, print the text on sentence strips and cut into individual word cards.

4. **Note:** You will need to enlarge a copy of blackline 1 for the cover *before* coloring. To make the cover, color, cut and glue the enlarged hot dog to a piece of 12″ x 18″ construction paper. Print the title, *I Like Hot Dogs.*

For the big book pages, color blacklines 1–18. Cut, leaving a small margin of white around each picture. Print the text on sentence strips. Glue the sentence strips and pictures on the 12″ x 18″ black or dark blue construction paper in the following manner:

cover   page 1   page 2

Contact or laminate all the pages and bind with three loose leaf rings.

5. Color, cut and mount the pictures from blacklines 24–34 on 4″ x 5″ tagboard cards. Contact or laminate. Laminate any additional food pictures that you intend to use in the pocket chart also.

6. Prepare the following frames:

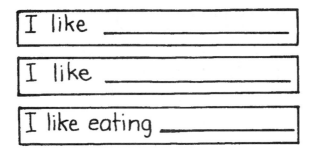

7. Cut two pieces of butcher paper, each about six feet long. Print at the top of one, *Foods We Like – Yum, Yum!* and on the second, *Foods We Don't Like – Yuck, Yuck!* Save these for the extension.

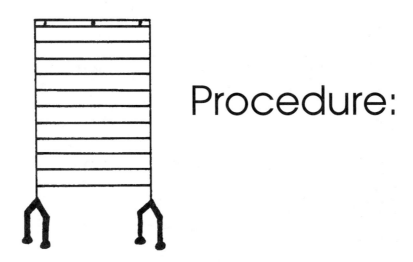

Procedure:

Note: *I Like Hot Dogs* is our rewrite of a poem by Karen Richardson, entitled *I Like.* This may be sung to the tune of *Twinkle, Twinkle Little Star.*

1. Use the big book to introduce *I Like Hot Dogs*, tracking the words as you sing. Sing again, using the *my turn, your turn* technique.
2. Sing a third time, placing pictures only in the pocket chart. Help the children discover the rhyming words in this song.
3. In the pocket chart develop the text, one line at a time. Using phonetic clues, have the children help you place the words in the correct order.
4. Reread the entire song from the pocket chart. Distribute all the words and pictures to the class and help them rebuild the song, using the big book as a guide. Sing to check for accuracy.

5. Begin a food wordbank by asking the children what foods they like. Print and illustrate these foods on the chalkboard. This wordbank needs to be saved so you will need to transfer these ideas to word cards. We have supplied you with a small collection of pictures to get you started. This wordbank will be expanded as the theme develops.

6. *Let's Eat* is a marvelous look at food from a child's point of view. We suggest you use this as a reference throughout this theme. At this time, discuss the pictures in the section *Favorite Foods* and see if there are any additional foods they would like to add to the wordbank.

7. To prepare for a rewrite of *I Like Hot Dogs*, print food words that are easily rhymed – such as soup, pie, bread, fish, cake, cheese, pears, bun, peach, etc. Help the children think of rhyming words and print these under each food word. (bread – head, dead, lead, shed, Fred, bed, sled, etc.)

8. Place the frames (prepared in step 6 under preparation) in the pocket chart and help the children create their own rhyming verses. The following were done by one of our kindergarten classes:

I like pizza – I like pie,
I like eating under the sky.

I like celery – I like soup,
I like eating in a group.

I like crackers – I like cheese,
I like eating under trees.

These verses may be saved in a variety of ways. You may wish to copy them on chart paper; the children may illustrate the verses in a class book or these may be put into an envelope and used as a pocket chart activity.

Extension: *Yum and Yuck Homework*

Homework: Ask the children to bring in two pictures of food – one that they like and one that they do not like. These will be used to make charts in which the children will compare and contrast various foods. If you wish to send a note, it might read as follows:

Dear Parents,

We are beginning a theme on food. Please help your child draw or cut two food pictures from a magazine – one your child likes and one your child doesn't like. This homework is due tomorrow. Thank you for helping.

Sincerely,

When the homework is returned, the children glue their pictures to the appropriate piece of butcher paper. Label each picture. When this is completed, ask the children what they notice about the two charts. Do they agree with everything that is on both charts? Lead the children to contrast and compare the two charts – isn't it interesting that peas are on both charts? How did that happen? etc.

Activity 2

Today Is Monday

Materials:

Materials needed:

- *Today is Monday,* by Eric Carle
- *Wednesday Is Spaghetti Day,* by Maryann Cocca-Leffler
- *More Spaghetti I Say!,* by Rita Golden Gelman
- *On Top of Spaghetti* (big book)
- *Strega Nona,* by Tomie de Paola
- Sentence strips
- Felt pens
- Blacklines 35–41 for the individual booklets
- 9″ x 12″ construction paper– various colors, seven per child, for booklet pages
- White yarn for the booklet cover, 12 inches per child
- One dozen stringbeans
- 6″ paper plates, one per child, for spaghetti page
- One package of spaghetti
- 6″ x 9″ red construction paper, one per child, for spaghetti sauce
- Dry alphabet soup pasta
- Brown corduroy – 4″ square, one per child, for roast beef
- Tempra paints for fish page and bean prints
- Sponges for sponge painting
- Tongue blades, one per child, for chicken drumsticks
- Tissue paper, shades of brown and tan for chicken

- 5″ construction paper squares, assorted colors, two per child, for the ice cream
- Clear glitter for the ice cream
- Blacklines 42–43 for the pocket chart
- Eight pieces of 5″ x 6″ tagboard cards for the pocket chart
- Butcher paper for a bulletin board
- Laminating film or contact paper

 Preparation:

Individual Booklets:

1. Duplicate the following blacklines in this manner:
   (Every child will need one of each item.)
   - blackline 35 on any light color construction paper
   - blackline 36 on tan construction paper
   - blackline 37 on brown construction paper
   - blackline 38 on white or manila construction paper
   - blackline 39 on white or manila construction paper
   - blackline 40–41 on white ditto paper
2. Cut brown and tan tissue paper into 1″ squares.
   These will be used to resemble skin on the chicken drumstick.
3. Cut each 4″ square of corduroy into a roast beef shape.
4. Cut white yarn into 12 inch pieces – one strand per child.
   (This will be used for the cover.)

Pocket chart:

5. Color, cut and mount blacklines 42–43 on 5″ x 6″ tagboard cards.
   Contact or laminate.

6. On sentence strips, print **Today is** two times. Print each day of the week three times and the food items one time. Print the phrase, beginning with **All you hungry** and ending with **eat it up** one time. (Copyright prevents us from giving you the entire text.)

7. If you choose to use the big book, *On Top of Spaghetti*, here are two places that carry this book:

The Big Book Bin
2570 Cyril Street
P.O. 8000
Abbotsford, B.C. V2S 6H1

Whole Language Resources
P.O. Box 426
Hilmar, California, 95324

Either one will need to be colored and laminated.

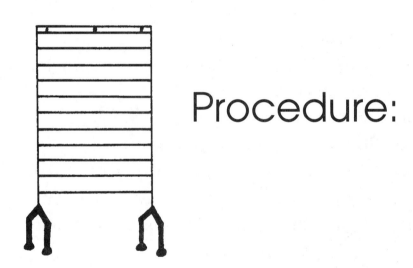

Procedure:

1. Read and enjoy *Wednesday Is Spaghetti Day*. The illustrations in this book are hilarious and we encourage you to spend some time discussing and predicting as the story unfolds. At the end of the book, the cats are anticipating Thursday, because Thursday is *Guacamole Day!*

Ask the children to tell you the names of the other days of the week and place these wordcards in the pocket chart as they are mentioned. Now check to see if the sequence is correct. (Your calendar is a great resource for this.) The children make any necessary corrections and read or chant. Remove these cards from the pocket chart.

2. Tell the children you have a book and song about different foods and the days of the week. Introduce *Today Is Monday* with the book. The words and melody are printed on the last two pages. Sing several times, helping the children learn the melody.

3. Sing the song again, placing the days of the week wordcards in the pocket chart in the following manner: Using a ten row pocket chart, place **Monday** in the eighth row, **Tuesday** in the seventh row, **Wednesday** in the sixth row, etc. Leave the first, ninth and tenth rows empty for now.

   Ask the children if they can remember what the special food was for each day. The children then match the picture cards with the appropriate days of the week. Refer back to the book to check for accuracy. Read or chant – *Monday, stringbeans. Tuesday, spaghetti. Wednesday, etc.*

4. Using phonetic clues, help the children match the food word-cards to the appropriate pictures and chant or read again. Now, distribute all the words and pictures to the children and have them find their partners and rebuild in the *same pockets.*

5. Ask the children if the whole song is now in the pocket chart. As the class tells you the missing phrases, add them to the pocket chart. Sing. An illustration of the completed poem can be seen on the next page.

Today is	Sunday	Today is	Sunday
Sunday		I__ ____
Saturday		C____
Friday		E__ ___
Thursday		R__ ___
Wednesday		Z____
Tuesday		S____
Monday		S____

All you hungry ____
____ ___ eat it up.

Note: As each new day is added, place that particular wordcard directly on top of the previous one.

6. Read *Strega Nona,* by Tomie de Paola. This is a very funny story about pasta. The children will enjoy creating their own magic words along with the three kisses.

7. For closure, sing *On Top Of Spaghetti* using the big book. This song is learned quickly and will soon become one of your classroom favorites.

Extensions:

Class Booklet
Innovations
Bulletin Board
Pasta Activities

Class Booklet:

This booklet will take several days to complete as there are a variety of art projects connected with each page. Please note that we have included the text for the booklet pages on blacklines 40–41 but you may wish to have your children write the words. When the pages are completed, bind at the top.

Cover – Each child needs one copy of blackline 39. The children complete the illustration by adding facial features and hair and coloring the clothing and plate. To make the spaghetti, each child will need one piece of white yarn (12 inches long). Make a small hole on the mouth and another small hole in the middle of the plate. Poke one end of the yarn through the mouth hole and knot it on the back side of the cover  cover. Repeat for the hole in the plate, taping this knot down on the back side of the paper. Place the yarn on the plate to resemble spaghetti. The fun begins when the yarn is pulled from the back side of the mouth hole and it looks like spaghetti is being slurped!

Page 1 – Each child will need one piece of 9″ x 12″ construction paper (any color). Using a green bean and green tempra, the children make 6 or 8 prints. When dry, add the words as shown in the illustration.

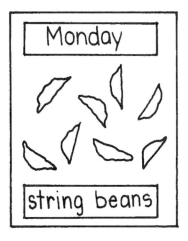

13

Page 2 – Each child will need one piece of 9″ x 12 " construction paper (any color), one 6″ paper plate, one piece of 9″ x 6″ red construction paper and a small mound of cooked, cooled spaghetti. Cut the red construction paper to resemble spaghetti sauce and glue this to the paper plate. Glue the paper plate to the construction paper page. Place a small mount of spaghetti on the red construction paper. The starch in the spaghetti will act as glue and adhere the pasta to the paper. Let this dry completely! Add the words as shown in the illustration.

Page 3 – Each child will need one piece of 9″ x 12″ construction paper (any color), one bowl from blackline 35 and a small handful of dry alphabet pasta. The children color the soup in the bowl, cut the bowl out and glue the bowl to the construction paper. Carefully glue the alphabet pasta to the soup and illustrate steam. Add words as shown in the illustration.

Page 4 – Each child will need one piece of 9″ x 12″ construction paper (any color), one place setting from blackline 38 and a pre-cut piece of corduroy to represent roast beef. The children color the place mat, silverware and plate. Cut and glue this placemat to the large construction paper page. Glue the corduroy to the plate and add the words as shown in the illustration.

Page 5 – Each child will need one piece of 9″ x 12″ construction paper (any color). Prior to assembling this page, the children will need to sponge paint a 9″ x 9″ piece of construction paper. We like to use at least two or three colors in the sponge painting. When this is dry they may draw a fish shape on the back of the sponge painting, cut the fish shape out and glue it on the large construction paper page. Illustrate crayon features to the fish and add the words as shown in the illustration.

Page 6 – Each child will need one piece of 9″ x 12″ construction paper (any color), one drumstick from blackline 37, one tongue blade, and a handful of pre-cut brown and tan tissue paper. Cut the drumstick shape. Using a pencil, the children wrap the tissue paper around the eraser end of the pencil, dip it in glue and place it on the brown construction paper drumstick. Continue until the drumstick is covered, making it look like fried chicken. Glue this to a tongue blade to complete the drumstick and then glue the drumstick to the construction paper page. Add words as shown in the illustration. When the tissue paper is flattened, it takes on the appearance of fried chicken.

Page 7– Each child will need one piece of 9″ x 12″ construction paper (any color), one cone from blackline 36, two pieces of 5″ square construction paper (representing their choice of ice cream flavors) and glitter. The children cut the cone and glue this down to the construction paper page. Cut out two ice cream scoop shapes and glue this to the top of the cone. Add clear glitter and the words as shown in the illustration.

Bulletin Board – Divide your bulletin board into seven spaces. Cut the letters and label the top and the bottom as shown in the illustration. Use the same ideas as listed in the booklet pages, only enlarge the items to fit the size of your bulletin board. The children will love to use this bulletin board to sing the song *Today is Monday.*

Monday	Tuesday	Wednesday	Thursday	Friday	Saturday	Sunday
String Beans	Spaghetti	Zoooop	Roast Beef	Fresh Fish	Chicken	Ice Cream

Innovation – If you are doing this theme around a holiday, it is easy to substitute words for *all you hungry children* – all you scary goblins, all you fluffy bunnies, all you tricky leprechauns, all you pudgy snowmen, etc.

Brainstorm for foods that would be appropriate for that particular holiday and insert them in place of the stringbeans, the spaghetti, etc. First grade and up are able to complete individual rewrites while kindergarten is more successful with class rewrites. This sample from our class was done at Thanksgiving time:

Monday, turkey
Tuesday, mashed potatoes
Wednesday, corn
Thursday, fruit salad
Friday, stuffing
Saturday, sweet potatoes
Sunday, pumpkin pie

All you kindergartners
Come and eat it up!

Pasta Activities – Begin by reading the marvelous book, *More Spaghetti I Say,* by Rita Golden Gelman, and discuss the silliness of this story. Ask the children if spaghetti is a fruit or a vegetable and help establish that spaghetti is a type of pasta. Brainstorm for all the different kinds of pasta with which they are familiar. Have a variety of pasta available for the children to explore. You might wish to have the children bring in samples of their favorites to add to the collection: spaghetti, macaroni, shells, wheels, elbows, bows, vermicelli, rigatoni, noodles, salad macaroni, rotelle, fettuccini, linguine, lasagna, tortellini, radiatore, tripolini, gnocchi, etc.

Brainstorm on the chalkboard for:
    things you love with pasta ("I love it with tuna")
    places where you can eat pasta ("I can eat it on the grass")
    things in which you can eat pasta ("I can eat it in my house")
    things you can do in or on pasta ("I can hide in it")

Chant all of the brainstorming. Then, using the following structure and the brainstorming, help the children create their own innovations. The children first choose the pasta about which they would like to write and then fill in the structure from the brainstorming on the chalkboard. You might wish to compile a class book with all the first grade innovations. Kindergarten is able to do this as a class experience and you may wish to put this rewrite on a large chart.

_____, **(name of pasta)**
_____,
I love it,
I love it!

I love it with _____,
with _____,
and with _____.

I eat it on _____,
and I eat it in _____.

I can _____ in/on _____,
and _____ in/on _____.

_____,
_____,
I love it,
I love it!

Sorting and Classifying – You will want to sort and classify the macaroni before you color it so that the focus will be on attributes other than color. This activity can be done very effectively in small, cooperative groups. List all the different ways the children sorted the pasta: shape, size, diameter of holes, texture, holes or no holes, curves, etc.

Dye Pasta – In a large, freezer-weight, ziploc bag, place two tablespoons of rubbing alcohol and one half of a large bottle of food coloring. (You may wish to use less of the color blue as it gets a bit dark.) Fill the bag half full of pasta, seal tightly and shake vigorously. Dump the contents on newspapers to dry.

There are numerous ways to use this colored pasta. You may wish to make necklaces, create mosaic pictures, use as counting manipulatives for math, etc.

Pasta Tasting – Prepare spaghetti for your class or have your children help make it. We like to offer two or three types of sauces (marinara, alfredo, carbonara, pesto) and then graph the choices (we even use macaroni on the graph!).

Favorite Spaghetti Sauce						
Marinara	⊛	⊛	⊛	⊛	⊛	⊛
Alfredo	⊛	⊛	⊛			
Pesto	⊛	⊛	⊛	⊛		

Pasta Song – We first learned this action song about twenty years ago and have absolutely no idea where it originated. This song is sung to the tune of *Alouette.*

> Hot spaghetti, I like hot spaghetti.
> Hot spaghetti, it's the best for me.
>
> Have I got it on my chin?
> Yes, I've got it on my chin.
>
> On my chin? On my chin!
> Oh-h-h-h-h-h-h
> Hot spaghetti, I like hot spaghetti.
> Hot spaghetti, it's the best for me.

Continue, adding the words *shirt, pants, shoes, floor, walls*, etc., in place of *chin.* Point to the items as each one is sung.

Activity 3

The Doorbell Rang

Materials:

Materials needed:

- *The Doorbell Rang,* by Pat Hutchins
- *If You Give a Mouse a Cookie,* by Laura Joffe Numeroff
- Blacklines 44–45 for the booklet
- Twelve pieces of 9" x 12" light colored, construction paper name tags
- Yarn for the construction paper name tags
- Sentence Strips
- Felt Pens
- One dozen cookies, artificial or real
- Twelve paper plates
- Platter, large enough for one dozen cookies
- Push bell to use as a doorbell
- Oyster crackers – each child will need a dozen
- Napkins

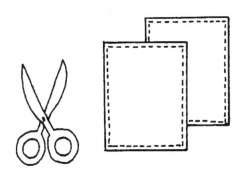

Preparation:

1. Duplicate blacklines 44–45, one per child, for the booklet. These blacklines need to be duplicated back-to-back. They must be positioned exactly as illustrated so the booklet may be folded in the correct sequence.

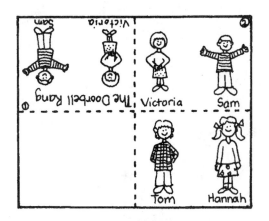

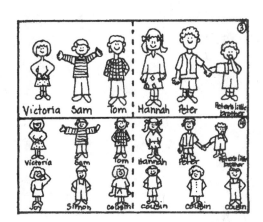

2. This needs to be folded exactly as illustrated and is too difficult for the children so the teacher will need to do it.

1st fold

2nd fold

3. On the twelve pieces of construction paper print the following (one name per paper):

Victoria	**Sam**
Tom	**Hannah**
Peter	**Peter's Little Brother**
Joy	**Simon**
Cousin	**Cousin**
Cousin	**Cousin**

Use the yarn, along with the above names, to create large name tags.

4. On a sentence strip print the following:

"No one makes cookies like Grandma," said Ma as the doorbell rang.

5. Print the following on sentence strips:

_____ stole the cookies from the cookie jar.
Who me?
Yes, you!
Couldn't be!
Then who?

6. Print the names of the children in your classroom on word cards.

Procedure:

1. Introduce this activity with the old chant, *Who Stole The Cookies?* Place the sentence strips in the pocket chart and have the names of your class ready for use. Start by placing a child's name at the beginning of the first line. The class reads or chants this question. The named child reads **"Who me?"** The class responds with **"Yes, you!"** The child denies with **"Couldn't be!"** The class then asks, **"Then who?"** Place the next child's name on top of the first and continue until all the children have had a turn.

   You may want to discuss the silliness of this chant with your class before-hand, as it is possible for a child to think the class is accusing them of taking cookies. This actually happened in one of our classes so we are very careful these days!

   Children can work with these pocket chart cards and will use them for months as an independent activity.

Joe	stole the cookies from the cookie jar
Who me?	
Yes you!	
Couldn't be.	
Then who?	

2. Tell the class that you have a wonderful story about cookies and you will need some volunteers to help dramatize it. Choose twelve children to take the parts of Victoria, Sam, Hannah, Tom, Peter,

Peter's Little Brother, Joy, Simon, Cousin, Cousin, Cousin and Cousin. Choose a child to ring the doorbell and another child to take the part of Grandma. The teacher will take the part of Ma.

Distribute the labels for the children to wear and give the push bell to the child who will ring the doorbell.

2. Introduce the book *The Doorbell Rang* by discussing the picture on the title page. The children will discover that Ma has made some chocolate chip cookies and that there are twelve of them. You may wish to elaborate on the meaning of a *dozen.* At this point the children will need to prepare a platter with twelve cookies for the dramatization.

3. Read the first page of the story to the children. Ask Victoria and Sam to get a paper plate and come and sit near you. Give the children the platter of cookies and ask them to "share them between yourselves." Before turning the page, ask each child how many cookies they have. Record this on the chalkboard (6 + 6 = 12) and have the class read.

4. Turn the page to read and check to see if our Victoria and Sam divided them the same as the children in the book. Continue reading and stop after the sentence, *"No one makes cookies like Grandma," said Ma as the doorbell rang.* A child needs to ring the doorbell now.

At this time, place the above sentence strips in the pocket chart and ask the children to read with you.
(**Note:** this will be repeated throughout the story.)

5. Continue dramatizing this story with each new arrival. The children will divide the cookies and the teacher will write the equation. The class will read this equation before turning the page.

6. At the end of the story, surprise the children with Grandma's platter of real cookies as a treat!

7. Reread all the equations from the chalkboard and discuss the different ways the children in the story were able to show twelve.

$$6 + 6 = 12$$
$$3 + 3 + 3 + 3 = 12$$
$$2 + 2 + 2 + 2 + 2 + 2 = 12$$
$$1 + 1 + 1 + 1 + 1 + 1 + 1 + 1 + 1 + 1 + 1 + 1 = 12$$

8. To develop the book further, have the children look at the cat, the stove, the floor, the stool and Ma's arms on each page. Discuss the subtle changes that occur throughout the book.

Extensions: *Individual Math Booklet*

*We would like to thank **Paula Ross**, a very dear friend and one of the finest first grade teachers we know, for this wonderful extension booklet.*

1. Distribute the pre-folded booklets to the children and a napkin with twelve small oyster crackers or bite-sized chocolate chip cookies.
2. Reread the story and with each ring of the doorbell, the children turn the page and divide their crackers or cookies for the new arrivals. First grade will record the equations on each page of the booklet. Kindergarten will chant them. Have fun eating!
3. For closure, read and enjoy *If You Give A Mouse A Cookie.*

Activity 4

Vegetable Garden

Materials:

Materials needed:

- *Vegetable Garden,* by Douglas Florian
- *Eating the Alphabet,* by Lois Ehlert
- *Let's Eat,* by True Kelley
- Blacklines 46–51 for *Tasting Time* booklet
- Sentence strips
- Felt pens
- Contact or laminating film
- Food wordbank cards from Activity 1
- Blacklines 52–55 for the pocket chart
- Sixteen 5″ x 6″ tagboard cards for mounting the pocket chart pictures
- Blackline 56 for a class book
- Fruits/vegetables for a tasting party
- Small paper plates and napkins

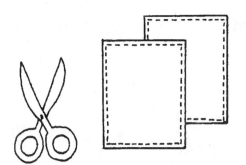

Preparation:

1. Duplicate blacklines 46–49, one per child.

2. Duplicate blackline 51 on manila construction paper, one per child. This will be the cover for the booklet.

3. You will need to duplicate blackline 50 several times. This page will become the cut apart work sheets the children will use. After you have decided on the foods that your class will be tasting, print each food name four times. Duplicate, one of each work sheet per child. (The actual number of work sheets will depend upon the number of foods that your class will be tasting.) We like to limit the tasting to eight fruits and vegetables.

carrot	carrot
carrot	carrot
apple	apple
apple	apple
tomato	tomato
tomato	tomato
pineapple	pineapple
pineapple	pineapple
leave blank	

4. For ease in this activity, we suggest that you assemble the booklets ahead of time. Each booklet will need a cover (blackline 51), one copy of blackline 46, one copy of blackline 47, one copy of blackline 48 and one copy of blackline 49. Staple at the top of each booklet. (Note: this booklet is designed for tasting eight different fruits/vegetables. If you would like to add more to this tasting activity, be sure to duplicate more pages.)

5. Print the following on sentence strips and then cut apart into individual word cards:

See the garden grow.
See the garden grow.
Fruits and veggies in a row,
See the garden grow.

6. Refer to the food wordbank that was begun in Activity 1. Make *two* individual wordcards for each fruit and vegetable. These will be used, along with the pictures, in step 2, under Procedure.
7. Color, cut and mount the pictures from blacklines 52–55 on 5″ x 6″ tagboard cards. Contact or laminate.
8. On sentence strips, print the fourteen phrases that correlate with the pictures from blacklines 52–55.
9. Duplicate blackline 56, one per child, for the class book.
10. On sentence strips, print the following:

We eat the stems of _____
We eat the leaves of _____
We eat the roots of _____
We eat the seeds of _____
We eat the fruits of _____

11. On sentence strips, print the following:

Grow above ground
Grow below ground

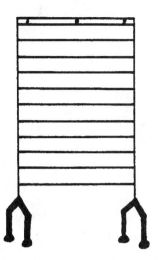

Procedure:

1. Ask the class if their family has ever had a vegetable garden. Discuss some of the things you have to do for successful gardening. Read and enjoy *Vegetable Garden*. List all the things that happened in this garden.

2. Place the pictures from blacklines 52–55 where they are easily accessible to the children. As you reread *Vegetable Garden*, the children take turns finding the appropriate pictures and then place them in the pocket chart.

3. Chant the poem, using pictures only, until it is memorized. Using phonetic clues, help the children match the phrases to the pictures. (**Note:** this book is excellent for working with letter sounds as all the phrases begin with consonants.) Read or chant.

4. Distribute all the pictures and phrase cards to the children and have them rebuild the poem in the pocket chart. Read or chant to check for accuracy.

5. Ask the children to help you gather the pictures from the food wordbank that grow either in the garden or the orchard. (This will make you aware of what the children actually know – especially if they suggest a picture of a hot dog!) You may wish to use *Eating the Alphabet* and/or *Let's Eat* as a reference for the children to validate their choices.

6. Place the following song in the pocket chart:

See the garden grow.
See the garden grow.
Fruits and veggies in a row,
See the garden grow.

This song is sung to the tune of *The Farmer In The Dell.* Sing several times, tracking as you sing, until the children have the song memorized.

The children may now take turns choosing differ-ent fruits and vegetables to take the place of the word garden. Place a picture directly on top of the word **garden** (in the first line), place the first wordcard directly on top of the word

See	the	🍎	grow.		
See	the	apple	grow.		
Fruits	and	veggies	in	a	row,
See	the	apple	grow.		

garden (in the second line) and place the second wordcard di-rectly on top of the word **garden** (in the fourth line).

7. To make a class songbook give each child one copy of blackline 56. The children refer to the wordbank for ideas. Depending upon the grade level, the children may either print in the missing word, print the entire structure or the teacher may take dictation. The children then illustrate at the top of the page. Bind, add a cover of your choice and sing. This will be a welcome addition to your class library.

8. Read and enjoy *Eating the Alphabet.* Discuss any unknown foods, referring to the Glossary at the back of the book for more infor-mation. Add the new foods to the wordbank.

9. **Sorting and Classifying.** Before beginning any sorting activity, you will need to develop the vocabulary of the categories and have reference books available to help answer questions that will

occur. (*Let's Eat* and *Eating the Alphabet* are two reference books we like to use.) We introduce this as a whole group activity using the pocket charts for the pictures and labels. At a later time, the children work in cooperative groups creating their own sorting and classifying rules. The children have great fun challenging the class to guess their rule. We are on occasion stumped as well – such as juicy and not juicy.

We suggest you begin with things that grow above the ground and below the ground. Place the labels in the pocket chart and have the children take turns placing the pictures under the appropriate label. Chant the entire sort when it is completed. (Potatoes grow below the ground. Radishes grow below the ground.) Also, orally develop sweet and not sweet with the pictures.

The other sorts we would suggest are fruits and vegetables, parts of plants we eat, etc.

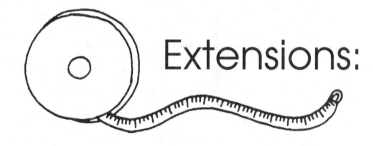

Extensions: *Tasting Party and Tasting Time Booklet*

Prepare eight plates, each with a different fruit or vegetable that is cut in bite-size portions. Each child will need a napkin and a paper plate. The plates will need to be passed around, one at a time, until each child has one of every food on their individual plate. You will be addressing each food individually; for example: ask the children to hold up their carrots. Discuss whether the carrot is a fruit or a vegetable. Where does a carrot grow? (above or below the ground) Is it sweet or not sweet? Lastly, eat the carrot and decide whether or not they like the taste. Continue in this manner with each of the eight foods.

Other questions that are relevant to tasting would include:
How does it feel in your hand? How does the food smell?
How does it sound when you chew it? How does it look?

The Tasting Time Booklets are the children's recording of the *Tasting Party*. For ease in making the booklet, display in the pocket chart the names as well as the pictures of the eight foods that were tasted. The children will work with one food at a time. For example: cut the four labels that say carrot and glue each label to the column of their choice on each of the four pages. For ease in making this booklet, help the children realize there are eight rows – one row for each of the foods.

like ☺	don't like ☹
carrot	
	tomato
apple	
	lemon
potato	

sweet	not sweet
carrot	
tomato	
apple	
	lemon
	potato

grow above ground	grow below ground
	carrot
tomato	
apple	
lemon	
	potato

vegetable	fruit
carrot	
	tomato
	apple
	lemon
potato	

There is a wonderful AIMS floating Fruit science lesson that is found in the 1984 edition of AIMS, pages 46–49. You can get information from: AIMS Education Foundation, P.O. Box 7766, Fresno, CA, 93747. We suggest you include vegetables as well as the fruits they list.

Activity 5

Stone Soup

Materials:

Materials needed:

- *Stone Soup,* by Ann McGovern
- *Growing Vegetable Soup,* by Lois Ehlert
- *Vegetable Soup,* by Jeanne Modesitt
- *10 Crunchy Carrots,* (big book) by Charlotte Diamond
- *10 Crunchy Carrots,* record or tape
- Ten raw carrots
- Blacklines 57–58 for the pocket chart
- Seven pieces of 5″ x 6″ tagboard cards for mounting the pocket chart pictures
- Blackline 59 for the class book
- Blackline 60 for the cover to the class big book
- Sentence strips
- 12″ x 18″ white construction paper for a class book
- Floor graph
- Paper bowls, plastic spoons and napkins
- Crock pot or large soup kettle
- Raw vegetables for printing
- 9″ x 12″ paper for printing
- Variety of raw vegetables that will grow into plants (potato, sweet potato, carrot, beet and lentils)
- Assortment of containers for growing vegetables

- Dishes, clay pots or coffee cans
- Sandwich-size bags
- Paper towels
- Lima beans

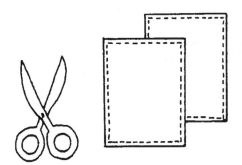

Preparation:

1. Color, cut and mount the pictures from blacklines 57–58 on 5″ x 6″ tagboard cards. Contact or laminate. Refer to *Stone Soup* for specific colors.

2. Print the phrase, **Into the pot went the,** on seven different sentence strips. Using *Stone Soup* as a guide, print each of the seven items that went into the pot on individual word cards. (round, gray stone, yellow onions, etc.)

3. Also print:

   Soup from a stone.
   Fancy that.
   The pot bubbled and bubbled.

4. To prepare the pages for the class big book, you will need 12″ x 18″ white construction paper. Make about four or five pages that look like this:

Into the pot went _____
Into the pot went _____
Into the pot went _____

5. Using the same size paper, prepare about four or five pages that look like this:

Soup from a stone.
Fancy that.
The pot bubbled and bubbled.

6. To make the last page, duplicate one copy of blackline 59. Color the table top and soup pot. Mount this in the center of the 12″ x 18″ paper and print **Soup from a stone** at the top and **Fancy that!** at the bottom. (Each circle will become one of the children in your class.)

7. To make a cover for this class book, duplicate blackline 60. Color, cut and mount on the cover page. Print the title.

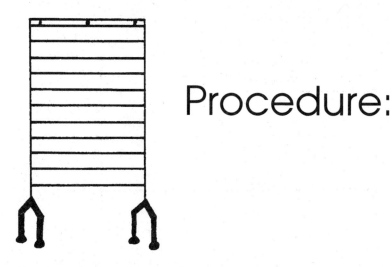

Procedure:

(**Note:** It is helpful if you completed Activity 4 prior to this lesson as your children will need information about vegetables. If you did not use Activity 4, you will need to spend some time developing facts concerning fruits and vegetables.)

1. Introduce the chant *10 Crunchy Carrots* by using Charlotte Diamond's big book. Chant it through several times to enjoy the rhythm and the fun found in the rhymes.

2. Ask the children to list all the things they have eaten that contain carrots: soup, stew, salad, cake, casseroles, etc. Tell the children that you have a funny story about a very different kind of soup that also is made with carrots. Read and enjoy *Stone Soup*. Most first graders will pick up on the humor right away but we have found that we need to help kindergarten children understand what the joke is.

3. Place all seven **Into the pot went the** phrase cards in the pocket chart. Using the book as a guide, help the children sequence the seven items that went into the pot. As each item is mentioned, place that picture in the pocket chart. Chant or read each item. (Into the pot went the round, gray stone. etc.)

4. Using phonetic clues, help the children place the labels next to the appropriate pictures. Read or chant.

5. Ask the children if they can remember what the little old lady said after each item was added to the soup. **(Soup from a stone. Fancy that.)** Add those to the next two pockets. Now ask the children what happened to the pot. **(The pot bubbled and bubbled.)** Add those words to the last pocket.

Into the pot went the	🥔	round grey stone
Into the pot went the	🧅	yellow onions
Into the pot went the	🥕	long thin carrots
Into the pot went the		_____
Into the pot went the		_____
Into the pot went the		_____
Into the pot went the		_____

Soup from a stone.

Fancy that.

The pot bubbled and bubbled.

6. Read the story from the pocket chart.
7. At a later date (the next day) begin the lesson by chanting *10 Crunchy Carrots*. Ask the children if they can think of another name for *Stone Soup* and try to elicit *Vegetable Soup*.
8. Read and enjoy the book *Growing Vegetable Soup*. You will need to discuss each page in addition to reading the text as a lot of information is contained in this story.
9. Ask the children if we wanted to make vegetable soup, would we have to grow it? Where could we find the ingredients? How many

of you like soup? Make plans to make *Stone Soup.* We like to send home a letter similar to this one in order to gather the fixings. This letter was sent prior to Thanksgiving, but could be adapted to any time of the year.

Dear Parents,

On Wednesday, November 22, the A.M. Kindergarten will be having a Thanksgiving Feast. The entree will be *Stone Soup.* It will be made out of whatever ingredients the children bring.

Each child will need to bring an ingredient on Wednesday, November 22nd. Some suggestions are listed below. Share this list with your child and help him/her choose one. It's OK if he/she chooses the one you've already got in the refrigerator!)

Thanks for helping,

carrot	eggplant	onion
tomato	green pepper	potato
celery	beet	squash
corn	peas	green beans
small can of tomato sauce		

10. You may wish to purchase soup starter or bring in additional spices, rice, barley, a soup bone, etc. to add to the soup. *Don't forget the stone!*

11. **Soup Day!** Before making the soup we like to graph the ingredients the children have brought. It is easy for the children to discover relationships if all the fixings are laid out on the floor. We suggest using a floor grid or making one out of a piece of butcher paper. Refer to *Mathematics Their Way* by Mary Baratta-Lorton, for information on developing real graphs.

You will want to have three or four adults available to supervise the cleaning and cutting of the vegetables. The children enjoy chanting, "Into the pot went the _____" as they add their own contribution. Be sure to start the soup early in the day as some vegetables take longer to cook.

Right before we sit down to eat we like to read the delightful book, *Vegetable Soup*. There is a wonderful message about being reluctant to sample anything you have never eaten before and this may be helpful for some five and six year olds!

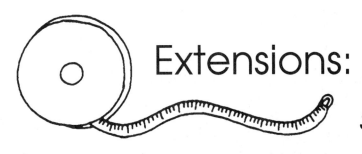

Extensions:
*Big Book,
Vegetable Prints,
Planting,
Subtraction Equations*

Class Big Book – While the soup is bubbling, help the children list all the items that they brought to put into the soup. Using coloring books and magazines the children search for pictures of the listed items. Those that cannot be found are illustrated by the children. The pictures are then glued to the prepared pages of the book. We like to alternate the pages so that the refrain, *"Soup from a stone. Fancy that. The pot bubbled and bubbled."*, appears after every three ingredients.

Into the pot went ~~~~ water Into the pot went 🫘 stone Into the pot went 🫛 peas

page 1

Soup from a stone Fancy that. The pot bubbled and bubbled

page 2

You may wish to laminate or contact this class big book and bind with loose leaf rings. You will find that this book will become one of the class favorites.

Vegetable Prints – It is fun to make placemats for the *Stone Soup* feast. Since these take a few hours to dry, we suggest making the prints the day before you plan to eat. We have had good luck printing with the following vegetables: potatoes, carrots, green beans,

40

onions, bell peppers and celery. Cut the vegetables in half so the children will be able to have a comfortable grip. Pour paint into pie tins or other shallow containers. We have found that dipping the vegetables into the paint is a disaster as there are blobs of paint all over and the prints are not clear. A method that is easier is for the children to use a brush to paint the printing end of the vegetables. These prints may be either random designs or simple patterns.

Planting – Very young children are able to easily grow and care for plants in the classroom. Since there is no guarantee that each plant will grow, it is best to grow more than one of each type of plant to insure success.

Potato – Choose a potato with many eyes. Stick three toothpicks in the sides of the potato about 1″ below the top. Put the potato in a tall jar so the toothpicks rest on the rim. fill the jar with water to cover the bottom half of the potato. Make sure the bottom is always in water. Once the eyes turn green, cut the potato into sections, making sure each section has at least one eye. Then plant the sections in soil and watch the potato plants grow. **Note:** You may wish to save this section of the extension for the next activity (One Potato, Two Potato).

Sweet Potato – Choose a potato with many eyes. Stick three toothpicks in the sides of the potato about one inch below the top. Put the potato, pointed end down, in a tall jar. fill the jar with water to cover the bottom half of the sweet potato. The plant will grow well in water and you should see roots in about ten days.

Beets and Carrots – Cut off the tops of several beets and carrots, leaving one inch of vegetable on each. fill a shallow dish with pebbles and water. Arrange the beet and carrot tops on the pebbles and put the dish in a light place that does not get direct sun. Sprouts should appear in about one week.

Lentils – Place a handful of dried lentils in a dish. Fill the dish with just enough water to cover the bottom. The lentils should not float in the water. Set the dish in a light place that does not get direct sun. Add enough water each day to keep the lentils moist. The lentils will begin to grow in about eight days. You will have a tiny lentil forest in about two weeks.

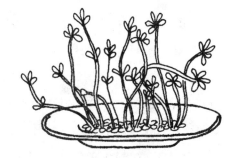

Lima Beans – It is fun for children to plant seeds and watch them grow. Each child needs to put a wet paper towel inside a small zip-loc bag. Place a few uncooked lima beans between the side of the bag and the paper towel. Seal the bag and keep in a warm place. Do not let the paper towel dry out. Soon the seeds will start to sprout. Look carefully and you will see something amazing. No matter which way you have put the seeds in the bag, the root grows down and the stem up. When the stem has grown about one inch long, you can plant the sprout outside or in a pot.

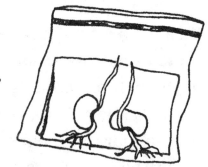

Subtraction Equations – After the chant *10 Crunchy Carrots* is memorized, it may be used to dramatize the concept of subtraction. Bring to school ten crunchy carrots and choose ten children to participate in the drama. As each verse is sung and dramatized, record the appropriate equation on the chalkboard and chant.

> **Ten crunchy carrots**
> **all yours and mine**
> **My gerbils ate one**
> **and now there's just nine.**
> **(10 – 1 = 9)**

First grade children may wish to record these equations on individual chalkboards. Enjoy eating the crunchy carrots after the drama is completed.

This chant is easily rewritten by the class. Brainstorm for a rhyming wordbank for each of the numbers, 1–10 or higher if you like. Brainstorm for who will eat the carrots and how many will be eaten each time.

Example:
> **Ten crunchy carrots**
> **lined up on the plate**
> **Mrs. Furuoka gobbled two**
> **and now there are 8.**
> **(10 – 2 = 8)**

Activity 6

One Potato, Two Potato

Materials:

Materials needed:

- *Bread And Jam For Frances,* by Russell Hoban
- *Jamberry,* by Bruce Degen
- Sentence strips
- Blacklines 61–62 for *One Potato, Two Potato*
- Seven pieces of 5″ x 6″ tagboard cards for mounting the above pictures
- Blacklines 63–65 for *Polly Put The Kettle On*
- Eighteen pieces of 4″ x 5″ tagboard cards for mounting the above pictures
- Blackline 66 for a class book page for *Jelly In A Bowl*
- Felt pens
- Contact or laminating film
- To set a table for four you will need the following eating equipment: plates, glasses, placemats, napkins, knives, forks, spoons, bowls, cup saucers, butter, salt and pepper shakers.
- Tea kettle (more than one is nice for comparison)
- For the tea party you will need:

  Ice Tea

  Sugar

  Bread – one slice per child

  Disposable cups, one per child

  Plastic spoons and knives, one per chi

  Paper plates, and napkins, one per chi

  Jelly – three or four different types

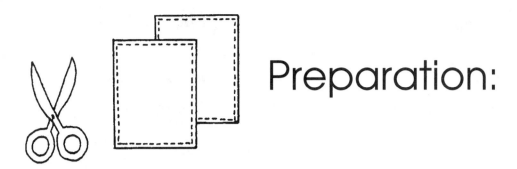

Preparation:

One Potato, Two Potato

1. Print the following rhyme on sentence strips and cut apart into individual word cards.

> **One potato, two potato,**
> **Three potato, four,**
> **five potato, six potato,**
> **Seven potato, more!**

2. On individual word cards, print the numerals 1 – 7.
3. Color, cut and mount the pictures from blacklines 61–62 on 5″ x 6″ tagboard cards. Contact or laminate.

Polly Put the Kettle On

1. Color, cut and mount the pictures from blacklines 63–65 on 4″ x 5″ tagboard cards. Contact or laminate.
2. On sentence strips print the following and cut into individual word cards:

> **Polly put the kettle on,**
> **Polly put the kettle on,**
> **Polly put the kettle on,**
> **We'll all have tea.**

3. You will also need to print: **spoons, forks, knives, napkins, plates, bowls, cups, glasses, salt and pepper, butter dish, saucers, placemats, breakfast, lunch, a snack** and **dinner**.

4. On individual word cards, print the names of all the children in your classroom.

Jelly In A Bowl

1. On sentence strips print the following and cut into individual word cards:

> **Jelly in a bowl,**
> **Jelly in a bowl,**
> **Wibble wobble, wibble wobble,**
> **Jelly in a bowl.**

2. Duplicate blackline 66, one per child, for the class booklet.

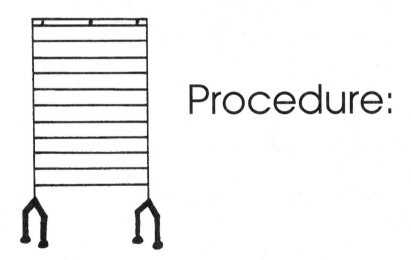

Procedure:

One Potato, Two Potato

1. Chant the nursery rhyme, *One Potato, Two Potato*, until the children have it memorized.

2. Chant again, placing the pictures from blacklines 61–62 in the pocket chart, one picture per line.

3. Children match the numeral cards to the pictures. Chant the poem again, tracking each line.
4. Using phonetic clues, the children match the number words with the numerals and pictures that are already in the pocket chart. Chant again. Help the children discover that the words **potato** and **more** need to be added to complete the poem.
5. Distribute all word and picture cards to the class and have the children rebuild the entire poem in the pocket chart. Read to check for accuracy.
6. As an extension, you may wish to do the potato planting from Activity 5.

Polly Put The Kettle On

1. Display several teapots and lead the children in discovering the various parts of the teapot – handle, spout, lid and whistle. You may wish to compare the shapes of the kettles. (Our experience tells us that many children are unfamiliar with a teakettle as many families rely on the microwave for heating water.) If time permits and you have the facilities, you might want to boil water in one of the kettles – perhaps timing this activity.
2. Brainstorm for uses of the water that is boiled in the kettle – tea, coffee, cocoa, soup, etc.
3. Introduce the song, *I'm A Little Teapot,* helping the children figure out ways to dramatize. A good friend, reading specialist Yvonne Ankele, shared the second verse to this old favorite with us. Thanks, Yvonne!

I'm A Little Teapot

I'm a little teapot, short and stout.
Here is my handle, here is my spout.
When I get all steamed up, hear me shout,
"Tip me over! Pour me out!"

I'm a little teapot, short and stout.
Here is my handle, here is my spout.
I can change my handle and my spout.
Just tip me over! Pour me out!

4. Introduce the nursery rhyme, *Polly Put The Kettle On,* chanting several times until the children have it memorized. Using phonetic clues, help the children build the first line in the pocket chart. For kindergarten, we like to use the pictures of Polly and of the kettle in place of the words. This way, the children only have three words to work with in the first three lines. The children will be able to build the following two lines independently by matching word to word. For the last line, use the same procedure as was used in the first line.

5. It is important to address the meaning of the contraction *we'll* that is found in the last line of the rhyme. Depending on the ability of your children, you may wish to do a lesson on contractions after this activity.

6. Distribute all picture and word cards to the class and the children will rebuild the entire rhyme in the pocket chart.

7. Orally brainstorm for other things that Polly could put on a table. The children will come up with a large variety of ideas that will be wonderful for sorting and classifying: food, utensils, decorative items, etc. (You may wish to refer back to the page on eating equipment in the book, *Let's Eat.*) Next, ask the children to think of things that Polly would get if she were setting the table for a meal. You will need to have your collection of eating equipment close at hand so that, as each new idea is mentioned, you are able to show that object. Then, place the corresponding picture in the pocket chart. (blacklines 64–65) **Note:** You will need to have available blank cards to quickly draw any items for which you have no picture.

8. Tell the children that we are going to see if we can do all the things that Polly would do if she were going to set the table. Using your class name cards, place one child's name directly on top of the word **Polly** and cover the picture of the kettle with a picture of placemats. Help the children read, *Lyn put the placemats on.* Lyn then gets the placemats and puts them on the table. Continue adding class names, pictures and dramatizing until the rhyme is complete. Read.

Now remove the names and pictures and repeat the above procedure, creating as many new verses as necessary, until all the materials have been used. To assure each child an opportunity to participate, we encourage you to clear the table and begin again as many times as necessary.

If questions occur concerning the table settings, let the children problem solve the solutions.

9. On additional days, the following classifications may be developed in the same manner: breakfast foods, lunch foods, dinner foods, snack foods. The only change you will need to make is to cover the word tea with the appropriate classification.

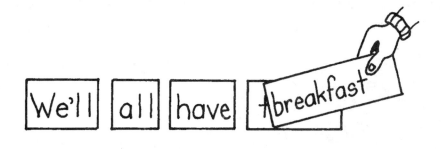

Jelly In A Bowl

1. Read and enjoy the wonderful book, *Jamberry*. Read again, asking the children to listen for all the different types of berries that are listed. As you read the children decide whether the berries are real or fantasy.

2. Discuss the difference between jelly and jam. Introduce *Jelly In A Bowl* orally. Add rhythmic motions and chant until the poem is memorized.

3. Use drama to develop the meaning of the words *wibble wobble*. Discuss what types of jellies might be in the bowl. Develop this chant in the pocket chart, line by line. Read.

4. To prepare for a rewrite, ask the children to name things to eat or drink, tell in what container the food would be served and give two describing words for each food. Divide your chalkboard into three sections and record the brainstorming.

5. Using the *Jelly In A Bowl* format, chant each of the brainstorming ideas in the following manner:

> Milk in a thermos,
> Milk in a thermos,
> Splish-splash, splish-splash,
> Milk in a thermos.

Here is a sampling from the creations of our five and six year olds:

Taco in a shell,
Taco in a shell,
Crinchy-crunchy, crinchy-crunchy,
Taco in a shell.

Coffee in a cup,
Coffee in a cup,
Jiggle-jaggle, jiggle-jaggle,
Coffee in a cup.

Corn dog on a stick,
Corn dog on a stick,
Hot and yummy, hot and yummy,
Corn dog on a stick.

Cereal in a bowl,
Cereal in a bowl,
Crackle- snap, crackle-snap,
Cereal in a bowl.

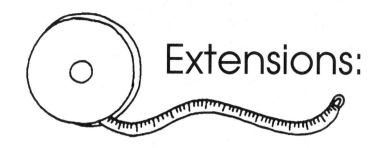

Extensions:

*Jelly In A Bowl
Class Book and
Tea Party*

Class Book – Using the brainstorming, along with blackline 66, the children create and record their own rhymes. After illustrating, the pages are bound together into a class book. This makes a delicious addition to your class library!

Tea Party – Prior to this party, you will need to make ice tea for your class. We would like the children to taste hot tea but the logistics of this, not to mention the safety element, make it difficult to implement in a classroom. We prefer to use a tea with no caffeine and our children seem to enjoy the herbal varieties better than plain tea.

A day or so before the party, the children need to make placemats – here is an opportunity to let the children apply the concept of pattern.

On the day of the party each child will set his or her place at the table. It is fun to sing or chant as each item is placed on the table:

> Let us put the placemat on,
> Let us put the placemat on,
> Let us put the placemat on,
> We'll all have tea.
>
> Now we put the plate on,
> etc.

You will need several containers of bread and jelly on the tables.
While the children are preparing their bread, pour the tea.
Once everyone has been served, chant together:

Jelly on the bread,
Jelly on the bread,
Wibble-wobble, wibble wobble,
Jelly on the bread.

Eat and enjoy!

At the end of the tea party, read the book, *Bread And Jam For Frances*.

Activity 7

Pease Porridge Hot

Materials:

Materials needed:

- *No Peas for Nellie,* by Chris L. Demarest
- *The Missing Tarts,* by B.G. Hennessy
- Blackline 67 for *Little Miss Muffet* make-a-play
- Blacklines 68–70 for *Little Tommy Tucker* pocket chart
- Blackline 71 for *Little Miss Muffet* pocket chart
- Nineteen pieces of 4″ x 5″ tagboard cards to mount all the pocket chart pictures
- 9″ x 12″ blue or green construction paper, one per child, for the play
- Tongue blades or popsicle sticks, one per child
- Black pipe cleaners, one per child, for the spider
- Brads, one per child
- Coarse black thread, about 10 inches per child
- Peas, fresh or frozen, about two or three per child
- Honey, in a squeeze bottle
- Plastic picnic knives, one per child
- Refrigerator biscuit dough (in a tube), one biscuit per child
- Jam or preserves, about a tablespoon per child
- Aluminum foil cut into about 6″ squares, one per child
- Cookie sheets

- Vinegar, one tablespoon
- Two cups of whole milk
- Soda crackers, one per child
- Sentence strips
- Felt pens
- Contact paper or laminating film

Preparation:

Pease Porridge Hot

1. On sentence strips print the following:

> **Pease porridge hot**
> **Pease porridge cold,**
> **Pease porridge in the pot,**
> **Nine days old.**
>
> **Some like it hot,**
> **Some like it cold,**
> **Some like it in the pot,**
> **Nine days old.**

Little Tommy Tucker

1. Print the following question and answer rhyme on sentence strips. Cut the first three lines into individual word cards, leaving the remainder as phrases. (**Note:** the first four lines are from the traditional nursery rhyme.)

> **Little Tommy Tucker**
> **Sings for his supper.**
> **What shall we give him?**
>
> **White bread and butter,**
> **Crackers and cheese,**
> **Burgers and fries,**
> **Carrots and peas.**
>
> **Tacos and rice,**
> **Meat and potatoes,**
> **Chili and cornbread,**
> **Lettuce and tomatoes.**
>
> **Cookies and milk,**
> **Eggs and ham,**
> **Cake and ice cream,**
> **Toast and jam.**

2. Color, cut and mount the pictures from blacklines 68–70 on 4″ x 5″ tagboard cards. Contact or laminate.

3. This rhyme is easily made into a big book by enlarging the blackline pictures and printing the words. Please note that you will need three pages of *Little Tommy Tucker, Sings for his super. What shall we give him?* This question will be inserted between each four line answer.

page 1

page 2

page 3

page 4

page 5

page 6

Little Miss Muffet

1. Print the following on sentence strips. Cut apart into individual word cards.

> **Little Miss Muffet**
> **Sat on a tuffet,**
> **Eating her curds and whey.**
> **Along came a spider,**
> **Who sat down beside her,**
> **And frightened Miss Muffet away.**

2. Color, cut and mount the pictures from blackline 71 on 4" x 5" tagboard cards. Contact or laminate.
3. Duplicate blackline 67, one per child, on white or manila construction paper.
4. Cut each black pipe cleaner into fourths.

Procedure:

Pease Porridge Hot

1. Place the sentence strips in the pocket chart and chant until the rhyme is memorized. Discuss with the class the meaning of the words *pease* (archaic plural of pea) and *porridge* (hot cereal).
2. Have the children find a partner and teach the rhythmic motions to this poem.

Pease   porridge   hot   Pease   porridge   cold

Pease   porridge   in the   pot   nine   days   old

3. Discuss with the children how they eat peas at their homes.
   Do they find it difficult to capture all the rolling peas?
   What kind of ways do the children use to "trap" the runaway peas?
   Tell the children that you have a special way to keep peas in place.
   Squirt a small amount of honey on the blade of a plastic knife.
   Place two or three peas on the honey.
   Now teach this hilarious jingle:

> I eat my peas with honey.
> I've done it all my life.
> It makes the peas taste funny,
> But it keeps them on my knife!

4. Ask the children if they would like to try it. Stand back and enjoy the fun!
5. Read the book, *No Peas For Nellie*, which deals with one of life's typical problems in a humorous way.

Little Tommy Tucker

1. Teach the following portion of the nursery rhyme, *Little Tommy Tucker.*

> Little Tommy Tucker
> Sings for his supper.
> What shall we give him?
> White bread and butter.

2. Line by line, build the rhyme in the pocket chart using words and the picture. Chant or read.
3. Discuss with the children the meaning of singing for one's supper. Do you think this happens today?
4. This rhyme is easily extended using favorite foods in a question-answer format. To further develop the activity in the pocket chart, the last line (White bread and butter) needs to be moved down one line, thus separating the question portion from the answer.

5. Now add the next three lines and pictures to complete the first answer portion of the rhyme. Children chant or read the question and answer from the pocket chart.

6. Track the first three lines again and then develop the next four answer lines. Read or chant and continue in the same manner with the last four lines.

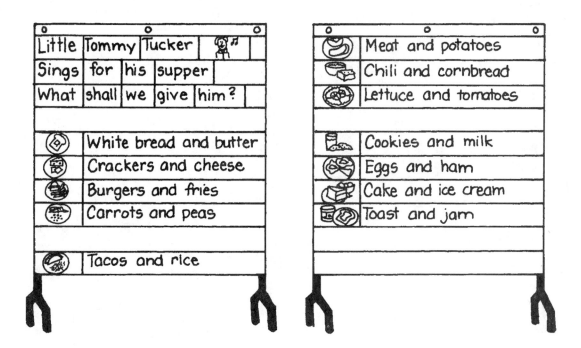

7. Divide the class into a question section and an answer section and have the entire rhyme read. The complete rhyme may also be read by having individual children read separate lines of the answer section and the entire class reading the repetitive question section.

8. Children will have fun using the noun wordbank to create many more four line answer sections.

Little Miss Muffet

1. Teach the rhyme, *Little Miss Muffet*. Many children will come to class already familiar with this nursery rhyme and the remainder will easily learn it with three or four repetitions.
2. Chant the poem again, placing the pictures in the pocket chart as you go.
3. This rhyme is wonderful for dramatization, which will help develop the meaning of the vocabulary. We suggest that the following words be discussed as the children attempt dramatization: tuffet, curds and whey, spiders and frightened.
4. To develop the meaning of *curds and whey,* stir two cups of whole milk over medium heat until it starts to bubble. Remove from the heat and add one tablespoon of vinegar and continue stirring until curds form. (Using a glass container makes it possible for the children to observe the change in the milk.) Strain off the whey, squeezing out any remains with a spoon. Serve on salted crackers. Children are surprised to discover that curds taste very much like cottage cheese. The whey is very bitter.
5. Using phonetic clues, develop the rhyme in the pocket chart, line by line. Read or chant.
6. Distribute all the wordcards and pictures to the class. The children rebuild the rhyme. Read again.

Extension: *Little Tommy Tucker, Little Miss Muffet and The Missing Tarts*

Little Tommy Tucker – a first grade class rewrite. Print the following on sentence strips, place in the pocket chart and read.

> **_____ doesn't like to eat _____.**
> **He/She would rather eat _____.**
> **He/She would rather eat _____.**
> **He/She would even rather eat _____.**
> **But, _____ doesn't like to eat _____.**

Introduce the above structure filling in the blanks with your name and your likes and dislikes:

> Mrs. Furuoka doesn't like to eat broccoli.
> She would rather eat spaghetti.
> She would rather eat pancakes.
> She would even rather eat escargo.
> But, Mrs. Furuoka doesn't like to eat broccoli.

Brainstorm with the children for things they do like to eat, listing each item on the chalkboard. Next brainstorm for things they do not like to eat.

Doesn't like	Like
spinach	ice cream
broccoli	cookies
liver	cake
squash	hamburgers
oysters	french fries

Help the children orally create many different versions of this structure using their names. First graders may then create their own interpretations and illustrate. Bind together into a book and enjoy the hilarity of this newest addition to your library.

Kindergarten children will enjoy participating in the oral portions of this extension, but the writing is difficult for this age child.

Little Miss Muffet – Make a Play

Give each child four pieces of black pipe cleaner, one piece of coarse black thread, one tongue blade, one brad, a piece of 9" x 12" green or blue construction paper and one copy of blackline 67. The children color and cut the picture of Miss Muffet and the tuffet. Fold the construction paper in half. Glue the tuffet and attach the brad as shown.

finished

Glue Miss Muffet to a tongue blade. To make the spider, begin by twisting two pieces of pipe cleaner together. Add the remaining pipe cleaners, one at a time, twisting each one as it is added. To finish the spider, bend the legs in a realistic manner. Tie a piece of coarse black string around the middle of the spider and wind the other end of the string around the brad.

Have the children chant the rhyme, using the stick puppet and the spider to dramatize the action.

The Missing Tarts – As a culmination activity for the nursery rhymes in Activities 6 and 7, read and enjoy *The Missing Tarts*. Many familiar Mother Goose characters join in the search for these missing pastries. This is a delightfully illustrated story and one that is easily predicted.

Of course it wouldn't be complete unless the children made tarts. Here is our quick and easy recipe for this delicious pastry.

① Pat pastry into shell (refrigerator biscuit)

② Get 1 T. preserves (or jam)

③ Put preserves in center of pastry shell

④ Put foil with shell on a cookie sheet

⑤ Bake at 350° until golden

⑥ Eat and enjoy!

Activity 8

Munch, Munch, Munch

Materials:

Materials needed:

- *The Biggest Sandwich Ever,* by Rita Golden Gelman
- *Bread Bread Bread,* by Ann Morris
- *Sam's Sandwich,* by David Pelham
- Blacklines 72–77 for the big book
- Blackline 78 for the pocket chart
- Six pieces of 4″ x 5″ tagboard cards for mounting the pocket chart pictures
- Blacklines 79–81 for individual booklet pages
- Sentence strips
- Felt pens
- Laminating film or contact paper
- Seven pieces of 12″ x 18″ construction paper for the big book
- Loose leaf rings for the big book
- Five different types of bread for tasting
  (bagel, tortilla, pretzel, croissant, wheat bread)

Preparation:

1. For the big book, print the following on sentence strips:

Peanut butter and jelly
Munch, munch, munch
I think I'll have it for my lunch.

Ham and cheese
Munch, munch, munch
I think I'll have it for my lunch.

Pickles and pastrami
Munch, munch, munch
I think I'll have it for my lunch.

Mustard and bologna
Munch, munch, munch
I think I'll have it for my lunch.

Tuna fish salad
Munch, munch, munch
I think I'll have it for my lunch.

Lettuce and tomato
Munch, munch, munch
I think I'll have it for my lunch.

2. For the big book, color, cut and mount the pictures from blacklines 72–77 on any color of 12″ x 18″ construction paper. Glue the sentence strips on the construction paper. The completed page will look like this:

cover

page 1

Continue in the same manner with all six pages. For a cover, print *Munch, Munch, Munch* on a piece of construction paper. Laminate or contact all the pages and bind together with loose leaf rings.

3. Color, cut and mount the pictures from blackline 78 on 4″ x 5″ tagboard cards. Contact or laminate.

4. For the pocket chart, prepare the following on sentence strips and cut apart into individual word cards:

> **Peanut butter and jelly**
> **Munch, munch, munch**
> **Peanut butter and jelly**
> **Munch, munch, munch**
> **Peanut butter and jelly**
> **Munch, munch, munch**
> **I think I'll have it for my lunch.**

Now print each of the following three times each and cut apart into individual word cards:

Ham and cheese

Pickles and pastrami

Mustard and bologna

Tuna fish salad

Lettuce and tomato

5. Duplicate blacklines 79–80, one per child, for the booklet.
6. On white or manila construction paper, duplicate blackline 81, one for every two children. (This blackline contains the cover and the back page.) Cut in half vertically.

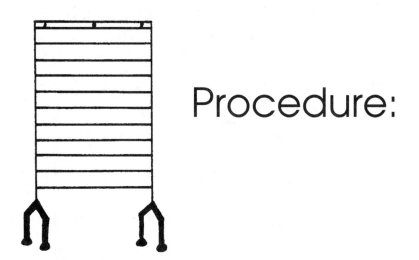

Procedure:

1. Introduce this activity with the big book, *Munch, Munch, Munch.* The text may be sung to the tune of *Skip To My Lou.* Sing from the big book, repeating the first two lines three times and the last line only once.

Example: Peanut butter and jelly
              Munch, munch, munch
              Peanut butter and jelly
              Munch, munch, munch
              Peanut butter and jelly
              Munch, munch, munch
              I think I'll have it for my lunch

2. Sing again, having the children join in where they are able.
3. Develop the first verse in the pocket chart one line at a time.
   Chant or read. As each new verse is developed, simply place the
   name of the new sandwich directly on top of the previous one.

4. Brainstorm for other kinds of sandwiches and sing again, using
   the new ideas. (Cream cheese and sprouts, chicken salad, roast
   beef, strawberry jam, grilled cheese, etc.)

5. It is fun to add pages to the big book using the ideas and illustrations of the children. Use the same format as you did in preparing the pages for the big book.

6. To add some humor, read the book *Sam's Sandwich*. (Sam has added some humorous condiments to his sandwich!)

7. Discuss with the children the kinds of breads that are used in making sandwiches and whether they think children all over the world would use the same type of bread that they do. Read *Bread, Bread, Bread* to help develop content. The index at the back of the book describes each type of bread pictured in the book and tells the country from which it comes. The children are always surprized to learn that pizza, pretzels and tortillas are also bread. Allow adequate time for discussion.

8. To extend this concept, you may wish to have a tasting session. The choices of breads listed under materials are optional. Choose your five favorites and cut these up into bite-sized pieces. Encourage the children to taste each of the five and graph the results.

Extensions: Individual Booklets and The Biggest Sandwich Ever

Individual Booklets – Review the kinds of sandwiches the children brainstormed earlier. Add to these ideas other sandwich makings such as mustard, mayonnaise, butter, lettuce, onions, tomatoes, pickles, sprouts, peppers, catsup, etc. To make the booklet, each child will choose his/her favorite sandwich. Distribute blackline 80 and, using one idea for each bread shaped page, have the children illustrate the four items they would like to put on their sandwich. The words are added at the bottom. Each child then needs to illustrate the entire sandwich between the two pieces of bread on blackline 81. (The top half of this blackline is the cover for this booklet.) Distribute blackline 79. The children can now cut out all ten of the bread shaped pages. The booklet is assembled in the following manner and stapled:

The Biggest Sandwich Ever – Read and enjoy this hilarious story about a little man who really does make the biggest sandwich ever. Ask the children if they think that we could make the biggest sandwich ever. We like to make a giant sandwich, with all the trimmings, and invite the parents to enjoy the feast. To begin with, contact the bread man at your local grocery store. Our bread man was able to furnish us with two loaves that were each six feet long. We requested that the loaves be sliced horizontally so that they were ready for making two giant sandwiches. Prior to sandwich day, send a letter home to each parent requesting a single sandwich ingredient. A sample letter is:

Dear _____,

    As part of our food theme, we are constructing *The Biggest Sandwich Ever!* To help us could you please send the following to school on Thursday? _____

    You are cordially invited to share our gigantic creation at 12:30 on Thursday in Room 3. Hope to see you then!

Thank you for your help!

Some of the things you may wish to request might include paper plates, cups, napkins, instant lemonade, chips, pickles, tomatoes, lettuce, onions, sliced ham, salami, bologna, turkey, roast beef, Swiss cheese, jack cheese, American cheese, cheddar cheese, mayonnaise and mustard. You will need to provide knives for spreading, something in which to mix lemonade and a sharp knife with which to cut the sandwich.

On sandwich day, the bread will arrive on boards. The children take turns adding their contributions. Those children who contributed paper items might wish to help spread mustard or distribute pickles. The important thing is that every child participates in creating this sandwich.

After the arrival of the parents, as an introduction you might wish to have your children read the book, *The Biggest Sandwich Ever*, and then unveil the real biggest sandwich ever! ENJOY!!

Activity 9

Going On A Picnic

Materials:

Materials needed:

- *The Teddy Bears' Picnic,* by Jimmy Kennedy
- *This Is The Bear And The Picnic Lunch,* by Sarah Hayes
- *Going On A Picnic* from *The Corner Grocery Store,* sung by Raffi (record or tape)
- Green and blue butcher paper for the bulletin board mural
- Tempra paints
- Newsprint
- Food for a picnic
- Paper plates, plastic utensils, cups and napkins
- Blankets to sit on for the picnic
- Camera and film

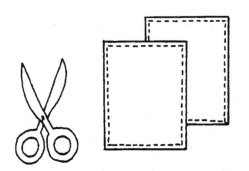

Preparation:

1. Contact your room mother and discuss how you wish to organize your picnic. You will need sandwiches, salad (we like macaroni), apples, melon, lemonade and cookies.

2. To prepare for the mural, staple to the bulletin board or wall blue butcher paper for sky and green butcher paper for the ground.

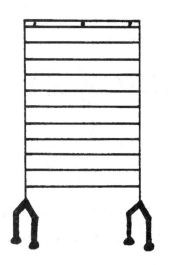

Procedure:

We would like to thank our good friends and fellow teachers,
Sue Rothman, Barbara Sarkany-Gore and Adrianne Egeland
for these innovative activities.

1. Read and enjoy the book, *This Is The Bear And The Picnic Lunch*.
2. Discuss picnics. What do you take? Where do you go?
   What do you do? When do you go?
3. Introduce the song, *Going On A Picnic* with the record or the
   tape of *The Corner Grocery Store*. Sing several times until the
   song is memorized.
4. **Picnic Day –** Have the following ready: sandwiches, salad, melon,
   apples, lemonade, cookies, blankets, cups, paper plates, plastic
   utensils, and napkins. Let the children help carry all the items
   to your picnic site. Sing the song *Going On A Picnic* as you walk.
5. You will want to take pictures of the children arriving at the
   picnic site, carrying the various food items mentioned in the
   song. You will also want to take some general picnic pictures.
   These photos will be used in making a class book of the song.
6. When you return from the picnic, read the timeless book,
   The Teddy Bears' Picnic. If you are fortunate enough to have
   the book with the recording, there will be lots of opportunities
   for drama.

Extensions:

Mural and Photo Class Book

Mural

1. Brainstorm for other foods you could take on a picnic and list these on the chalkboard.

2. Sing the song, *Going On A Picnic,* creating new verses with the children's ideas. (Did you bring the peaches? Yes, I brought the peaches. Did you bring the popcorn? Yes, I brought the popcorn. etc.)

3. Have the children help list all the things that are needed to create a mural of their version of the song, *Going On A Picnic.* (Clouds, sun, trees, flowers, shrubs, birds, kids in the class and the food they will bring to the picnic.)

4. Let some of the children illustrate the background (clouds, sun, trees, shrubs, birds, flowers, etc.) and cut these pictures out. Add these to the mural.

5. Each child needs to illustrate a picture of herself/himself carrying their favorite picnic food. Cut out the illustration and add it to the mural. If you have the room, print the question and answer sequence next to each illustration. If more that one child chooses the same item to bring, group these illustrations together.

6. The creations of this mural lend themselves to a class big book. Simply remove the illustrations and mount these, along with the words, on 12″ x 18″ construction paper. For the first three pages, you will need to print the first fifteen words, **Going on a picnic, leaving...** and have your children illustrate. For the very last page, print the last seven words, **Ready for a picnic, here...** and have a child illustrate. Sequence the pages of your book and bind. Sing and add to your class library.

Photo Class Book

1. A class book of the song, *Going On A Picnic,* may be created by using your photographs and the words to the song. Print the text on 9″ x 12″ construction paper, two sentences per page.
2. Glue the appropriate photo between the two sentences.

Activity 10 *Eggs For Tea*

 Materials:

Materials needed:

- *The Cake That Mack Ate,* by Rose Robart
- *Eggs for Tea,* by Jan Pienkowski
- *Too Many Eggs,* by M. Christina Butler
- Blacklines 82–83 for pocket chart of *The Cake That Mack Ate*
- Blackline 83 (bottom line) for a graph
- Blacklines 84–85 for pocket chart of *Eggs for Tea*
- Twenty-five pieces of 4" x 5" tagboard cards to mount the pocket chart pictures
- Six artificial eggs (hard boiled will do)
- Egg carton for half dozen eggs
- Small counting cups, one per child
- Jelly beans or small candy eggs, six per child
- Individual chalkboards, if available
- Sentence Strips
- Felt pens
- Contact paper or laminating film
- Potatoes (mashed, fried, baked and boiled) for tasting
- Paper plates and plastic utensils
- Butcher paper for creating a graph

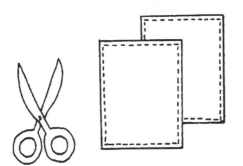

Preparation:

1. **Note:** blackline 83 contains three pictures needed for the pocket chart activity and four pictures that are needed for both a graph as well as the pocket chart. Duplicate one copy of blackline 83 and save it for future use. Duplicate an additional copy to be used for pocket chart pictures.
2. Color, cut and mount the pictures from blacklines 82–85 on tagboard cards. Laminate or contact.
3. To prepare the graph, color cut and mount the pictures from blackline 83 on a piece of butcher paper.

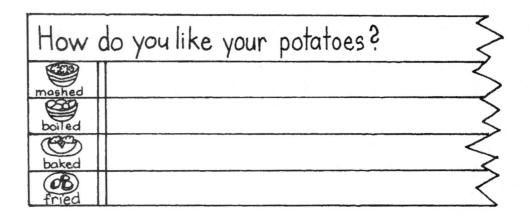

4. Prior to the tasting day, prepare a small portion of each of the four types of potatoes – mashed, boiled, baked and fried. These may be put into crock pots and be kept warm until time for tasting.

5. On individual word cards print the following: **cake, egg, hen, corn, seed, farmer, woman, candles, Mack.**

6. For the book *Eggs For Tea*, print the repetitive structure, found on the first four pages. It begins with *This little monster can't believe...*and ends with *...leaves ____ for you and me.* Leave blank spaces for the number words.
(Copyright prevents us from printing the entire structures for you.)
Print two sets of number cards, one through five.
(Use either numerals, words or a combination of both.)
Print only one copy of number six.
Print the five phrases that describe what each monster did with his egg. Begin with **He gobbles**... Also print **All gone!**

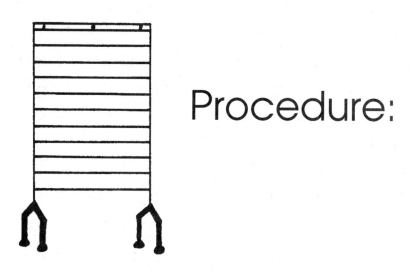

Procedure:

1. Introduce this activity with *The Cake That Mack Ate*. This is a humorous cumulative story of the demise of a birthday cake. After reading, discuss who is having a birthday.

2. Place the picture of the cake in the first line of the pocket chart and the picture of Mack in the ninth. Ask the children to name some of the things that had to happen in order for this cake to be made. As each item is mentioned, add that particular picture to the pocket chart – in the order that they are mentioned. You may have to give hints in order to get all seven items.

3. Discuss the sequence of the items and help the children place the pictures in the order of the story. Use the book to check for accuracy.

4. Chant the entire story from the pocket chart.

5. Using phonetic clues, help the children match the individual words to each line in the pocket chart. Read or chant again. Distribute all picture and word cards and rebuild the story by having the children find their partners and return the cards and pictures to the pocket chart.

6. Ask the children if this book reminds them of another well known story. You might want to read *The House That Jack Built* or *The Napping House*.

7. Discuss other ways eggs might be used besides as an ingredient in baking. Introduce the book *Eggs For Tea*. Read and enjoy. Dramatize during this first reading with the half dozen egg carton and the six artificial eggs. Individual children take turns being the monsters and the whole class dramatizes how they fix the eggs. Be prepared to discuss poached, boiled, fried and scrambled.

8. To develop this, place the repetitive structure in the pocket chart, leaving room at the left for the pictures and leaving the third line empty.

9. Help the children develop the repetitive structure six times, once for each monster. Each time you will change the monster picture, the numbers and the phrases telling how the monsters prepared the eggs. (Change these by merely placing the new words directly on top of the old ones.)

10. Before reading the story again, each child needs an individual chalkboard or blank paper and a counting cup with six small edible eggs. As you read the story once again, the children will use the eggs to create the subtraction equations and then record these equations on their chalkboards. At the end of this activity your hungry little monsters will enjoy gobbling up all their eggs for tea.

Extensions:

Rewrite and Graph

1. Recall the different ways that the monsters fixed eggs. Tell the children that there are other foods that may be prepared in a variety of ways. (Apples, tomatoes, hot dogs etc.) Another of these foods is potatoes. Brainstorm for ways to cook potatoes. (You will need at least four ways for the rewrite.) Print the new phrases on sentence strips. The brainstorming from one of our classes is:

> He swallows one up
> He mashes one
> He boils one
> He bakes one
> He fries one

   To rebuild this in the pocket chart, you will need to print the word **potatoes** to place over the word **eggs** in the structure.

2. Follow the previous *Eggs For Tea* procedure and rebuild this rewrite of the book in the pocket chart. Read or chant.

3. It is fun to have a small tasting party at the end of this activity. We brought samples of the four types of potatoes for the children to sample. This was followed by graphing their favorite.
   (**Note:** If you chose a different type of food for your rewrite, simply substitute that food for the tasting.)

4. As a culmination, read and enjoy, *Too Many Eggs*. Your class will love taking part in this delightful story by helping to count out the eggs, and at the end finding out how many eggs Mrs. Bear actually used.

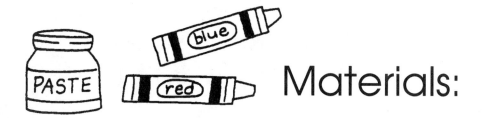

Activity 11

Potlock

Materials:

Materials needed:

- *Potlock,* by Anne Shelby
- *Aikendrum* Big Book
- Felt pens
- Contact paper or laminating film
- 12″ x 18″ white construction paper, one per child (first grade)
- Blackline 86 for drawing Aikendrum, one per child (kindergarten)
- Blackline 87 for the alphabet book
- Bulletin Board letters for children to trace
- Paper plates and napkins

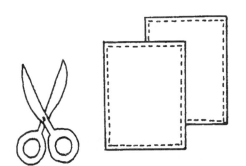

Preparation:

1. If you choose to use the big book, *Aikendrum,* here are two places that carry the text:

Whole Language Resources
P.O. Box 426
Hilmar, CA 95324
Phone (209) 668-4142

The Big Book Bin
2570 Cyril Street
P.O. 8000
Abbotsford, B.C. V2S 6H1

Either choice will need to be colored and laminated.

2. For kindergarten, duplicate blackline 86 on white construction paper, one per child for drawing Aikendrum.
3. Duplicate twenty-six copies of blackline 87 on white construction paper for the alphabet book.

Procedure:

1. Introduce this activity with the big book, *Aikendrum.* Sing several times until it is memorized. Kindergarten children love to add hand motions as they sing – for *in the moon,* they form a circle overhead with their arms, for *he played upon a ladle,* the children

pretend to strum a musical instrument and, for the remainder of the verses, the children point to the various parts of the head.

2. Children enjoy illustrating this song as they sing. We suggest giving each first grade child a piece of 12″ x 18″ construction paper and kindergarten children a copy of blackline 86. The first grade children will need to draw a large U shape, similar to that on blackline 86. We have found that this U shape (which represents the chin and sides of the face) helps establish a large size creation and also helps with the placement of the features.

   As the children sing each new verse, that particular food is illustrated. We like to do this along with our children.

Aikendrum

3. Informally rewrite the song. Sing again, this time pausing and asking the children what food they would like to choose for his hair. (And his hair was made of string beans, string beans, string beans, etc.) Continue in this manner with all the facial features. It is fun to add food items for the clothing Aikendrum might be wearing. (And his hat was made of watermelon, etc.) This is fun to illustrate also.

4. Discuss with the children the meaning of the word *potluck*. Read and enjoy the marvelous book, *Potluck*. This is a wonderful book for language development. Not only are there foods that might be new to the children but the alliteration used in the book deserves much discussion.

5. After the first reading, return to the beginning of the book and pose the question, "Why do you think Alpha and Betty set the table for 31 when there are only 26 letters in the alphabet?" To solve this, the story will need to be reread, counting the children as you progress. Have fun!

6. Suggest to the children that they could write their own alphabet book of foods. List all the letters of the alphabet on the chalkboard and brainstorm for foods. For the more difficult letters you may wish to use adjectives beginning with that letter. (Q – quick oats or quick rice, etc.) Save this for the alphabet book extension.

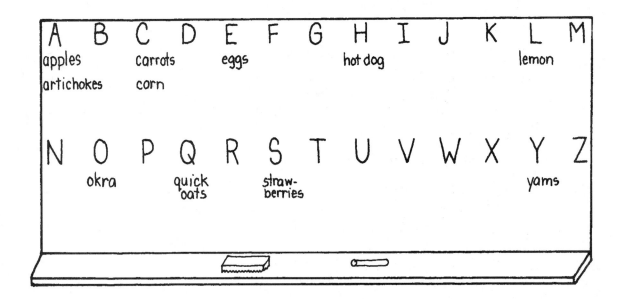

7. Chant each of the brainstormed items, *A is for apple. A is for artichokes.* etc.

Aikendrum Rewrite – If you would like to further develop *Aikend-rum,* the following structure may be used. Pick an alphabet letter with which to work and develop the structure orally. Continue in this manner with several letters and different animals. The following is an example from one of our classes:

There was a <u>cat</u> lived in a <u>cave</u>
And his name was <u>Calico</u>

And he liked to play the <u>clarinet</u>
And he liked to read <u>comic books</u>
And he liked to eat <u>corn dogs</u>
And he liked to wear <u>a great big coat</u>
And he liked to go to <u>concerts</u>

And his name was <u>Calico</u>

Alphabet Book – Each child chooses a different letter of the alphabet and is given that particular bulletin board sized letter. From the brainstorming the child then chooses a favorite food that begins with that letter. The child is given a copy of blackline 87 and traces the letter in the upper left hand corner (next to the word *is*). The page is completed by printing the food choice on the bottom line and then illustrating. It is fun to decorate the traced letter.

Depending on how many children you have, you may need to have some of the children prepare a cover, a title page, an authors page, etc. so that each child has an opportunity to participate. Collect all the pages and have the children help you sequence them. Bind into a book, read and add to your class library.

Potluck – What better way is there to culminate a food theme than to have a potluck? There are many ways to implement this...ours is just one way.

If you are fortunate enough to have room mothers, you will want to enlist their help. However, this potluck may be pulled off with the help of some older children. We like to send home a letter indicating the plans for the potluck several days in advance.

Dear Parent,

As a culmination of our food theme, we would like to end with (what else?) eating! At this time, it seems appropriate to eat our way though the alphabet. We would like to have a potluck on Friday, April 16. We are trying to gather foods that begin with each individual letter of the alphabet. Since there are 26 letters, we will only need a bite-sized portion of each food.

If you would like to participate, would you please send a food beginning with the letter _____. With the help of older students, we will prepare bite-sized portions of each food. To help us plan ahead and prepare for this potluck, would you please return the bottom portion of this page as soon as possible?

Mrs. Furuoka

_____

Yes! I would like to participate and will send food beginning with the letter _____ on Friday, April 16. _____

(parent signature)

After the responses have been returned, you will know which foods you might need to bring. Encourage inexpensive foods such as apples, carrots, lettuce, grapes, raisins, etc. so this will not become a burden to anyone.

On the big day, after the foods have been prepared, have the children help you set up a big buffet table. Label each food with the appropriate letter and chant them with your class. (A is for apple, B is for banana, etc.) Grab a plate, napkin and enjoy!

Optional Activities

Popcorn – Popcorn offers many opportunities for art projects as well as eating! Two books we like are *The Popcorn Book*, by Tomie de Paola, and *Popcorn*, by Frank Asch. Don't forget to let your children experience the science activities with kernels of corn in the book, *Science on a Shoestring*.

Your children will marvel as corn is popped in their test tubes! Another fun thing to do is to draw a large picture of an ear of corn on a large piece of tagboard. Have the children estimate how many pieces of popcorn it will take to cover the inside of the drawing. Count out in groups of ten, using counting cups and a place value board. Glue the popcorn directly on the tagboard. A helpful hint is to have a rule that when gluing, each piece of popcorn must touch another piece. You might want to have the children tally as the popcorn is counted.

Pancakes – A wonderful poem for the pocket chart is *Pancakes* by Christina Rosetti. Tomie de Paola's great book, *Pancakes For Breakfast*, is a wordless book that is excellent for sequencing. You will want to make pancakes and also make butter! These are the most fun when you use individual portion recipes.

Pizza – Begin with Charlotte Diamond's song, *I Am A Pizza*. This hilarious song is offered in big book form (The Big Book Bin) and is also found on one of her records. A book we like is *Little Nino's Pizzeria*, by Karen Barbour. To add some math activities, collect a variety of sizes of pizza boxes. Help the children seriate them. You will want to make individual pizzas (we like to use an English muffin as the dough) and graph your favorite kind. A field trip to a pizza parlor is great fun.

Grocery Shopping – *The Corner Grocery Store* is one of our all time favorite songs to use with this age child. It is found on a Raffi record with the same name. This song is easily made into a big book and is a must for a rewrite. *Tommy At The Grocery Store,* by Bill Grossman, and *I Want A Blue Banana,* by Joyce and James Dunbar, are fun books to read – both books deal with little ones at the grocery store. *Don't Forget the Bacon,* by Pat Hutchins, and *The Elephant And The Bad Baby,* by Elfrida Vipont, are both books that have wonderful repetitive phrases for pocket chart work. A field trip to the grocery store is easy to arrange. Also, math may be incorporated in your first grade classroom as you work with the concept of money.

The Big Block Of Chocolate, by Janet Slater Redhead, is a marvelous book about that most delicious taste of all – chocolate! Each of the characters in this book finds the block of chocolate and decides to save it for later. Your children will love the humorous ending! This book has an outstanding repetitive phrase that lends itself to the pocket chart as well as a rewrite using another type of food – how about peanut butter?

Gregory, The Terrible Eater, by Mitchell Sharmat, is another favorite with the children. This is a good book to read when you want the children to try new things. This is a great book to use when you are studying animals and discussing the various menus. It has also been developed on Reading Rainbow.

The Carrot Seed, by Ruth Kraus, lends itself to a pop-up book, as well as actually planting carrots. It is easily sequenced in the pocket chart and integrates well in a discussion of vegetables.

Bibliography

Although we have made every effort to locate the current copyright holders of the materials used in this theme book, some we were unable to trace. We will be happy to correct any errors or omissions.

Butler, M. Christina, *Too Many Eggs*, David R. Godine, Publisher, Inc., Boston, MA, 1988.

Carle, Eric, *Today Is Monday*, Philomel Books, New York, NY, 1993.

Cocca-Leffler, *Wednesday Is Spaghetti Day*, Scholastic, Inc., New York, NY, 1990.

Cole, Joanna, *Who Put The Pepper In The Pot?*, Parents Magazine Press, New York, NY, 1989.

Degen, Bruce, *Jamberry*, Harper & Row, Publishers, New York, NY, 1983.

Demarest, Chris L., *No Peas for Nellie*, Aladdin Books, Macmillan Publishing Company, New York, NY, 1988.

de Paola, Tomie, *The Popcorn Book*, Holiday House, New York, NY, 1978.

de Paola, Tomie, *Strega Nona*, Prentice Hall, New York, NY, 1975.

de Paola, Tomie, *Pancakes for Breakfast*, Harcourt Brace Jovanovich, Publishers, New York, NY, 1978.

Ehlert, Lois, *Eating the Alphabet*, Harcourt Brace Jovanovich, Publishers, New York, NY, 1989.

Ehlert, Lois, *Growing Vegetable Soup*, Harcourt Brace Jovanovich, Publishers, New York, NY, 1987.

Florian, Douglas, *Vegetable Garden*, Harcourt Brace Jovanovich, Publishers, New York, NY, 1991.

Gelman, Rita Golden, *More Spaghetti I Say!*, Scholastic, Inc., New York, NY, 1977.

Gelman, Rita Golden, *The Biggest Sandwich Ever*, Scholastic, Inc., New York, NY, 1980.

Grossman, Bill, *Tommy at the Grocery Store*, Harper Trophy, New York, NY, 1989.

Hayes, Sarah, *This Is The Bear And The Picnic Lunch*, Joy Street Books, Little Brown and Company, Boston, MA, 1988.

Hennessy, B. G., *The Missing Tarts*, Viking Kestrel – Viking Penguin Inc., New York, NY, 1989.

Hoban, Russell, *Bread And Jam For Frances*, Harper & Row, Publishers, U.S.A., 1964.

Hutchins, Pat, *Don't Forget the Bacon*, Mulberry Books, New York, NY, 1976.

Hutchins, Pat, *The Doorbell Rang*, Greenwillow Books, New York, NY, 1986

Kasza, Keiko, *The Wolf's Chicken Stew*, G.P. Putnam's Sons, New York, NY, 1987.

Kelley, True, *Let's Eat*, E. P. Dutton, New York, NY, 1989.

Kennedy, Jimmy, *The Teddy Bears' Picnic*, Green Tiger Press, La Jolla, CA, 1983.

Lord, John Vernon, *The Giant Jam Sandwich*, Houghton Mifflin Company, Boston, MA, 1972.

McCloskey, Robert, *Blueberries for Sal*, Viking Press, New York, NY, 1968.

McCully, Emily Arnold, *Picnic*, Harper Trophy, Harper & Row, Publishers, U.S.A., 1984.

McGovern, Ann, *Stone Soup*, Scholastic, Inc., New York, NY, 1986.

McMillan, Bruce, *Eating Fractions*, Scholastic, Inc., New York, NY, 1991.

Modesitt, Jeanne, *Vegetable Soup*, Aladdin Books, Macmillan Publishing Company, New York, NY, 1988.

Morris, Ann, *Bread Bread Bread*, Lothrop, Lee & Shepard Books, New York, NY, 1989.

Numeroff, Laura Joffe, *If you Give A Mouse A Cookie*, Harper & Row, Publishers, New York, NY, 1985.

Pelham, David, *Sam's Sandwich*, Dutton Children's Books, New Mexico, 1991.

Pienkowski, Jan, *Eggs For Tea*, Doubleday, New York, NY, 1990.

Robart, Rose, *The Cake That Mack Ate*, Little, Brown and Company, Boston, MA, 1986.

Rockwell, Harlow, *My Kitchen*, Greenwillow Books, New York, NY, 1980.

Shelby, Anne, *Potluck*, Orchard Books, New York, NY, 1991.

Veitch, Beverly and Harms, Thelma, *Cook And Learn*, Addison-Wesley Publishing Company, Menlo Park, CA, 1981.

Vipont, Elfrida, *The Elephant and the Bad Baby*, Coward-McCann, Inc., New York, NY, 1986.

Westcott, Nadine Bernard, *Peanut Butter and Jelly*, Dutton Children's Books, New York, NY, 1987.

Blacklines

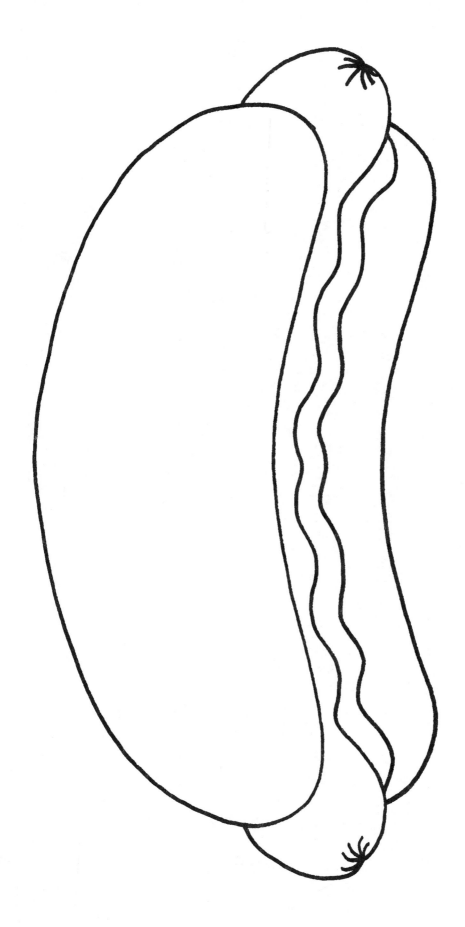

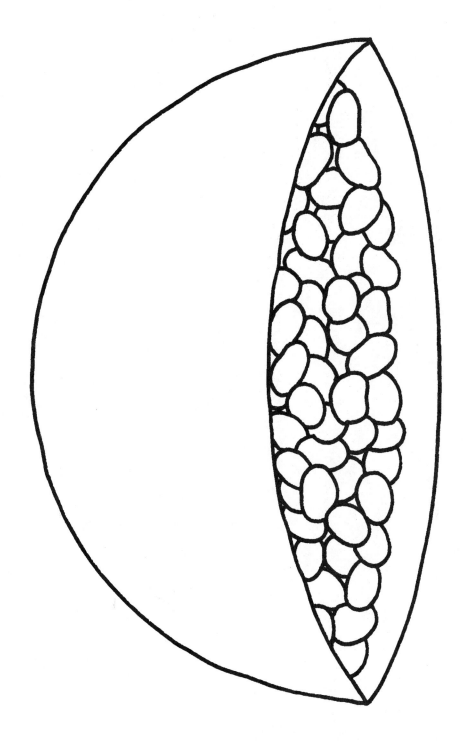

4

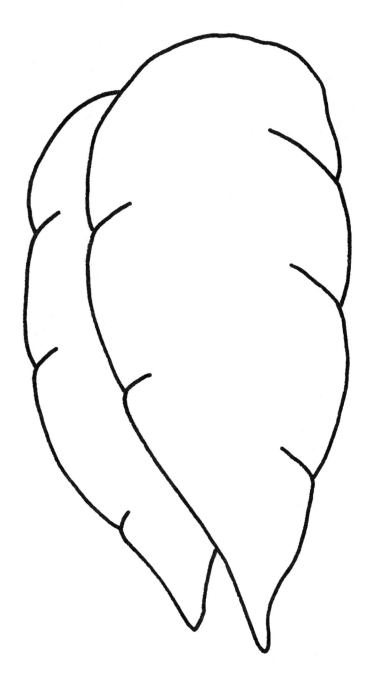

6

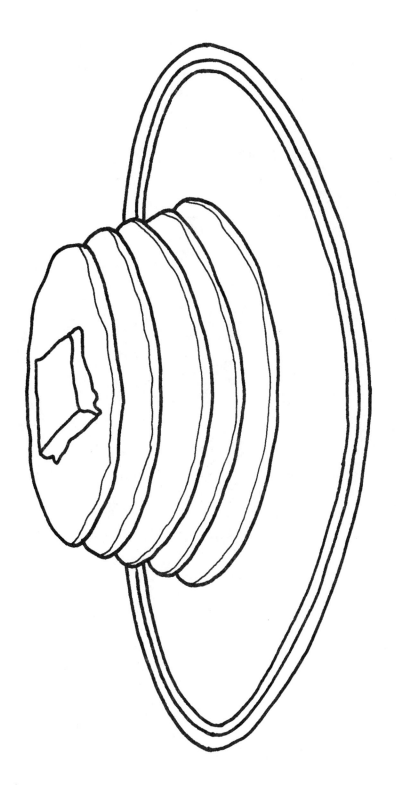

8

9

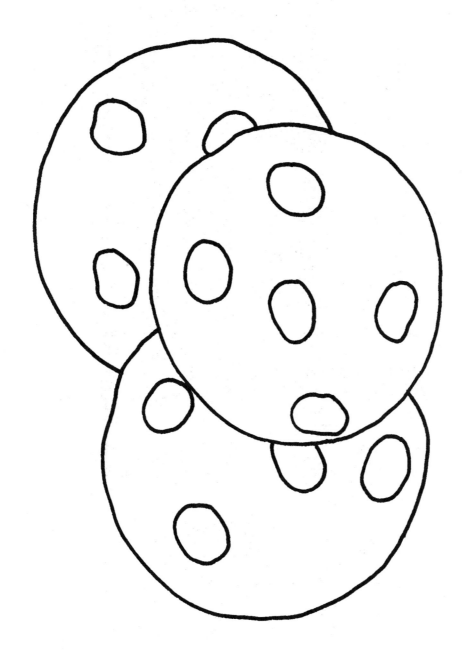

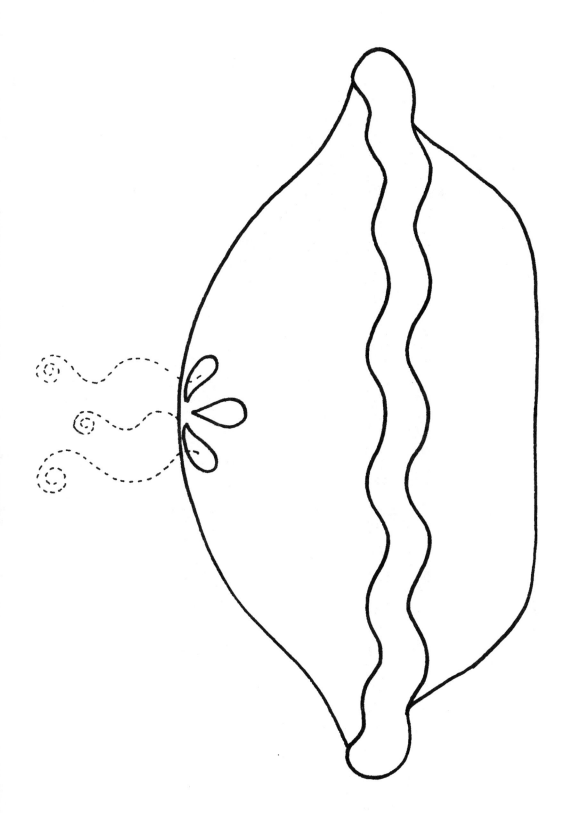

12

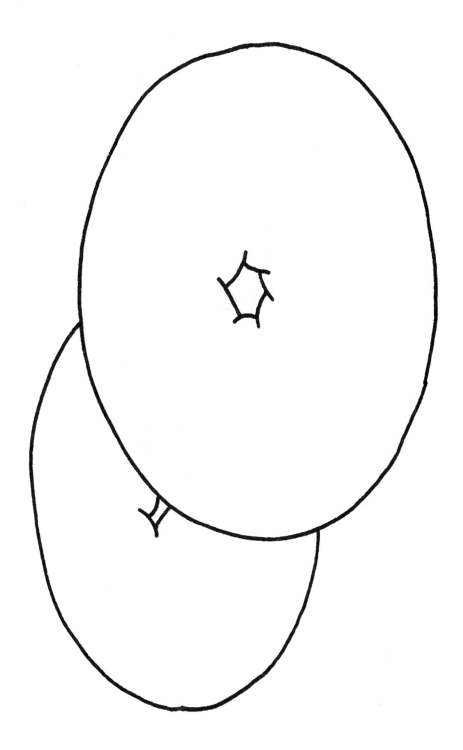

13

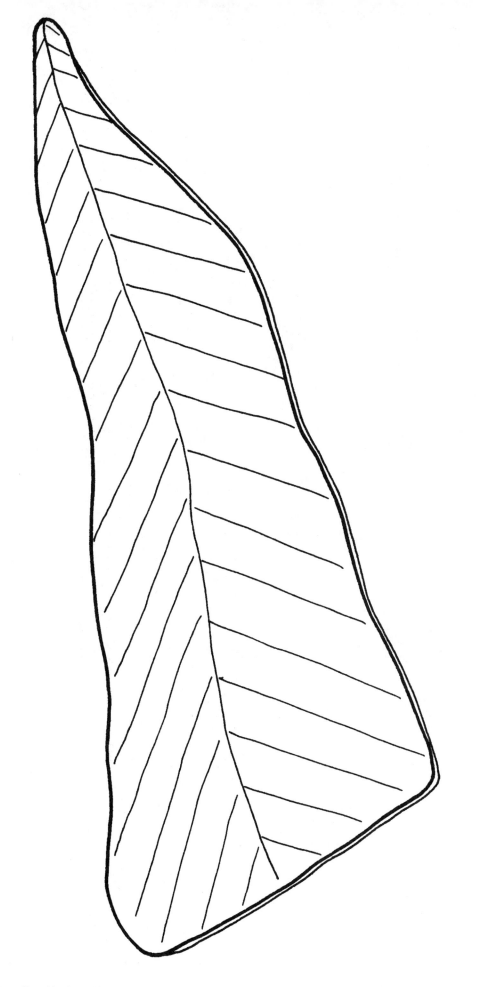

15

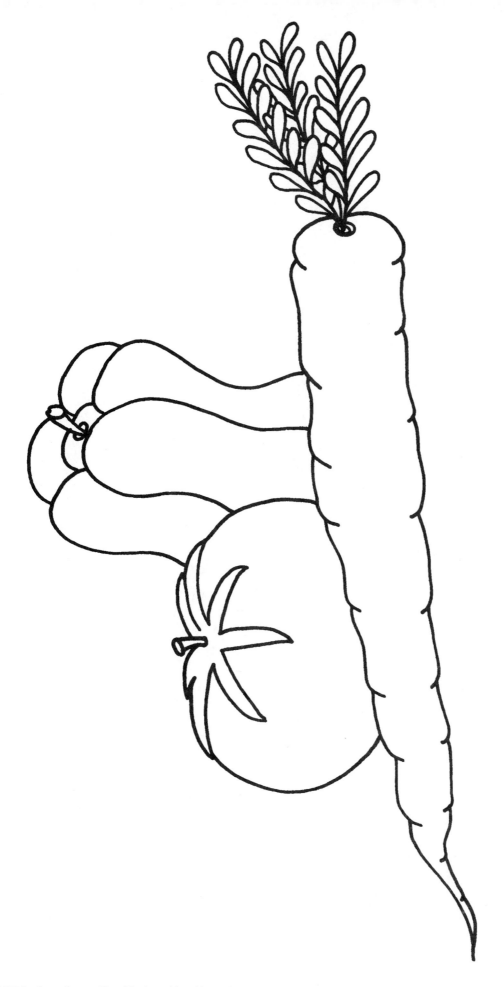

18

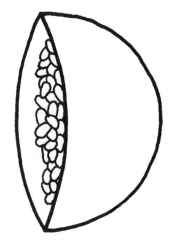

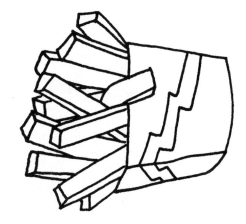

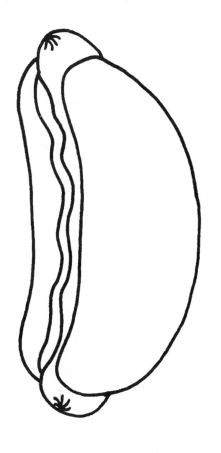

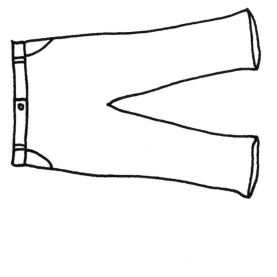

19

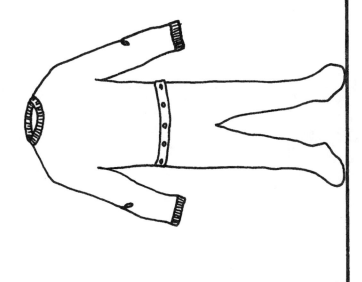

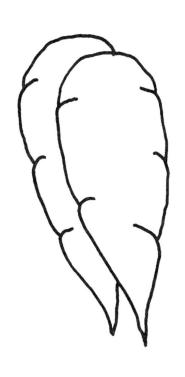

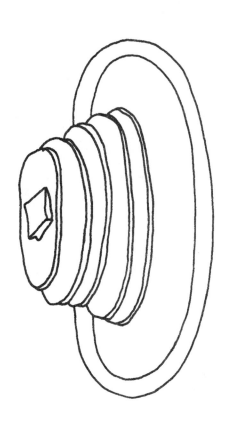

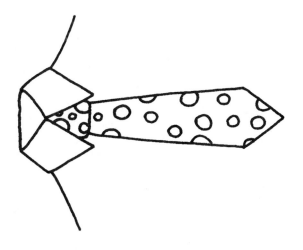

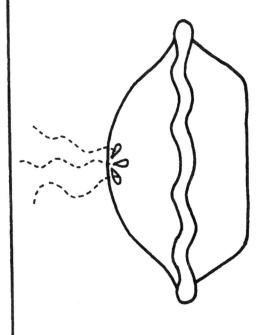

21

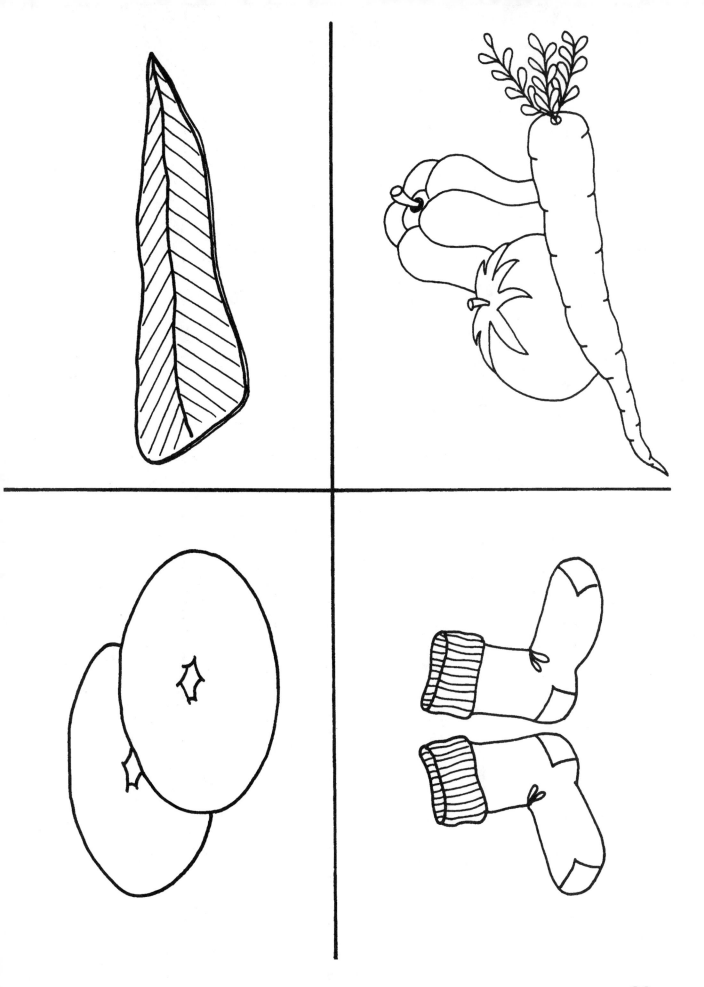

22

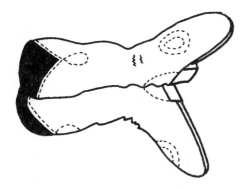

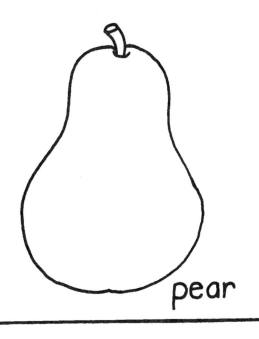

pear

peach

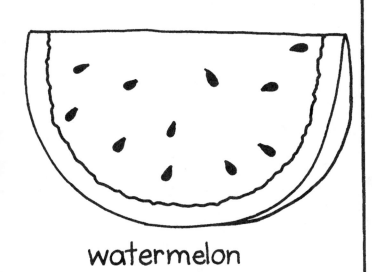

watermelon

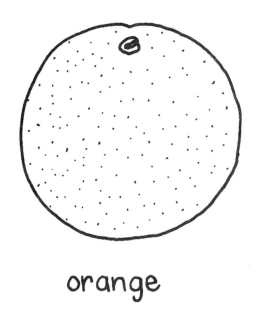

orange

cherries

raisins

pumpkin

pineapple

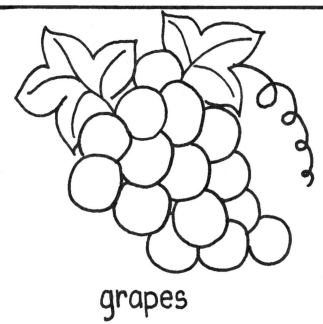

grapes

cantaloupe

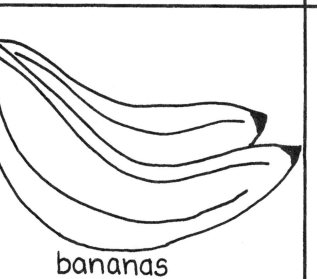

bananas

strawberries

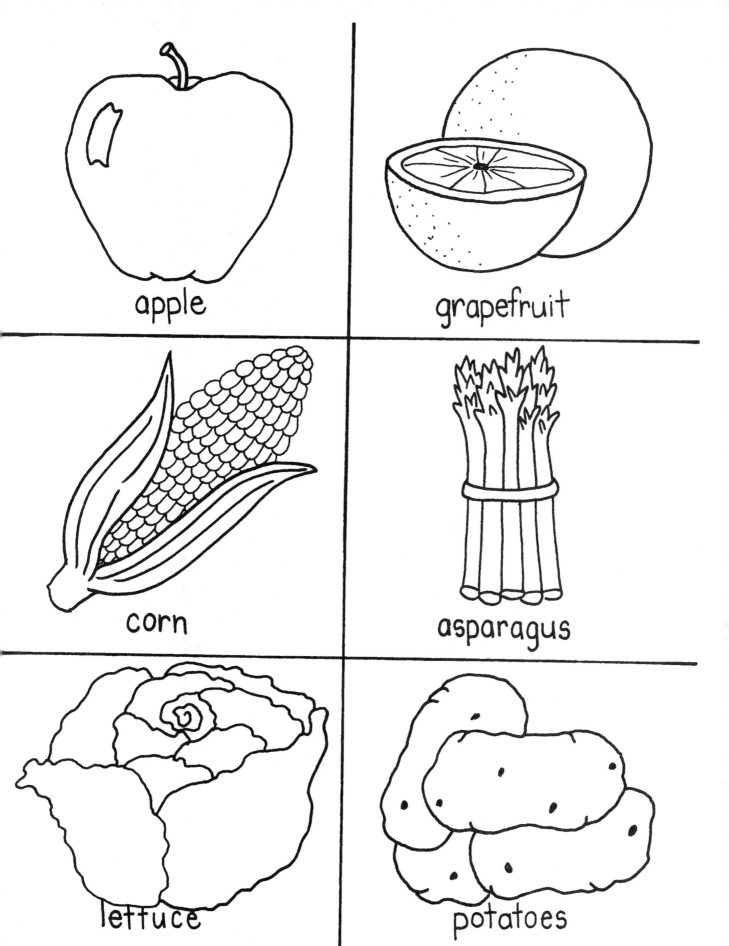

apple

grapefruit

corn

asparagus

lettuce

potatoes

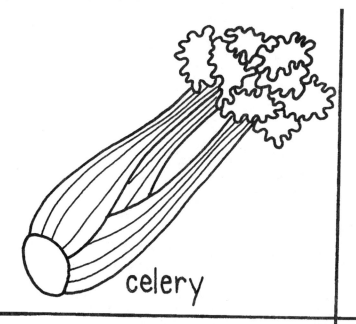

celery

tomato

green beans

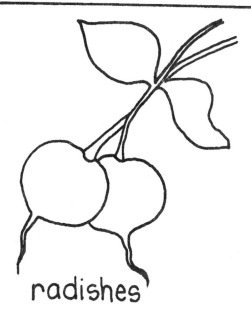

radishes

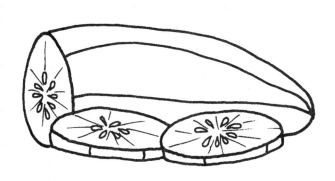

cucumber

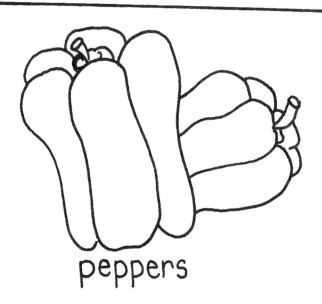

peppers

onion

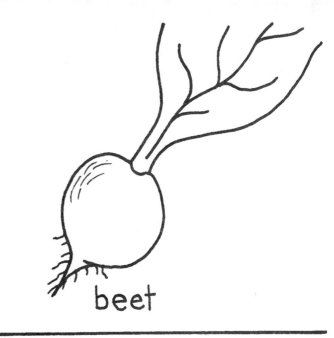

beet

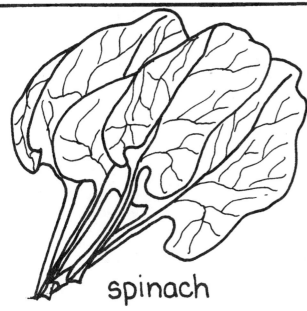

spinach

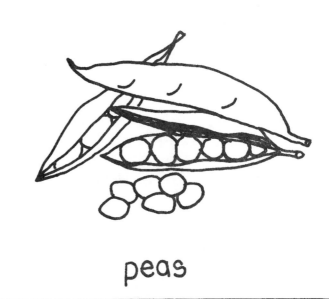

peas

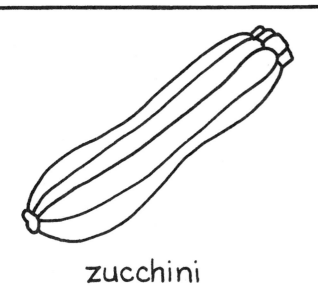

zucchini

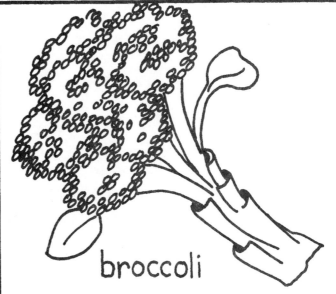

broccoli

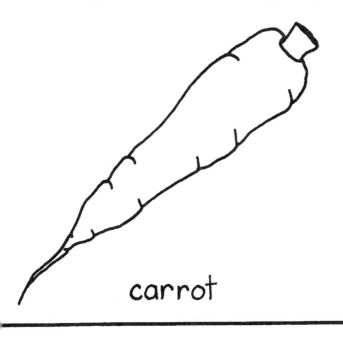

carrot

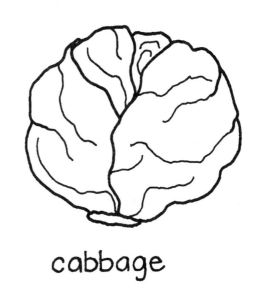

cabbage

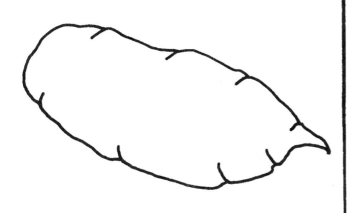

sweet potato

ground beef

tuna

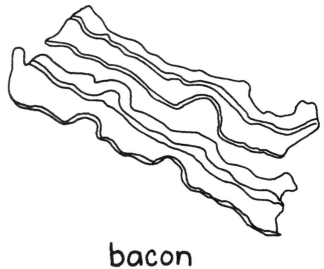

bacon

ham

hot dog

chicken

fish

corn tortilla

graham cracker

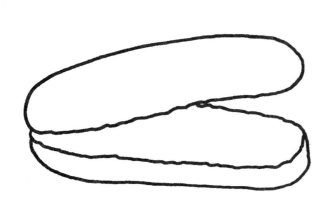

hot dog bun

bread

soda crackers

cereal

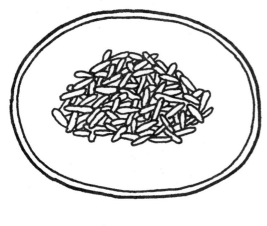

rice

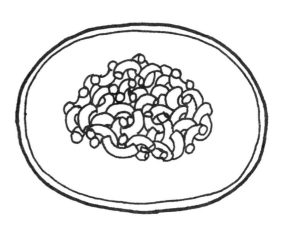

macaroni

spaghetti

oatmeal

pancakes

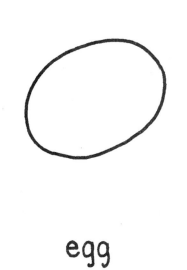

egg

cheese

butter

cottage cheese

ice cream

milk

peanuts

peanut butter

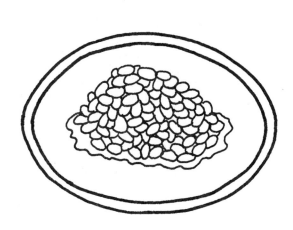

baked beans

black eyed peas

pinto beans

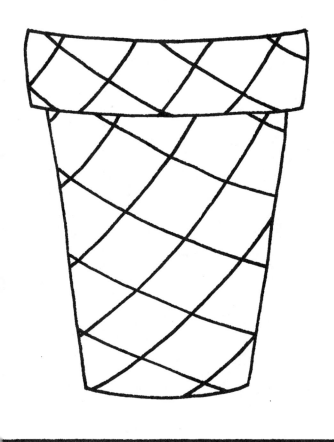
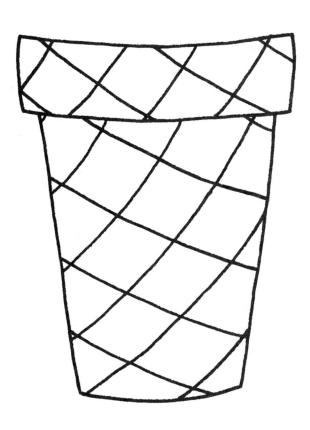
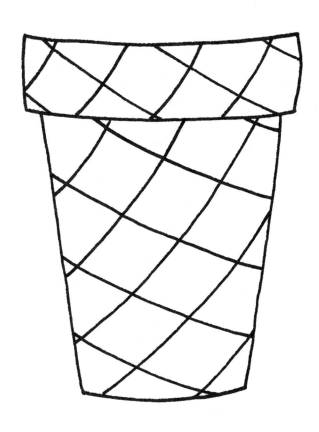

36

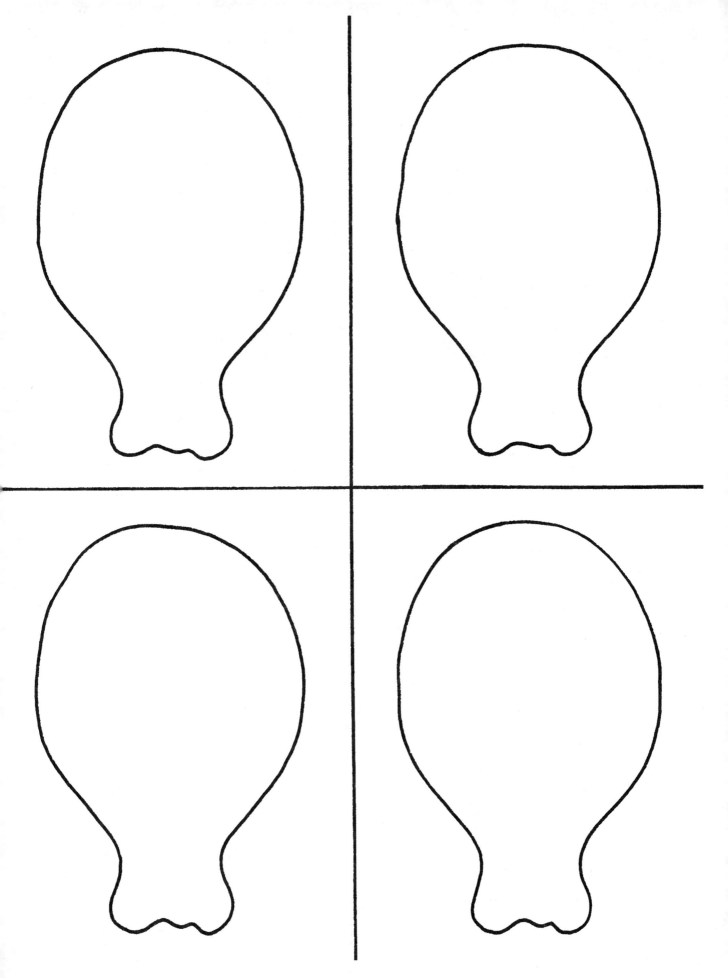

37

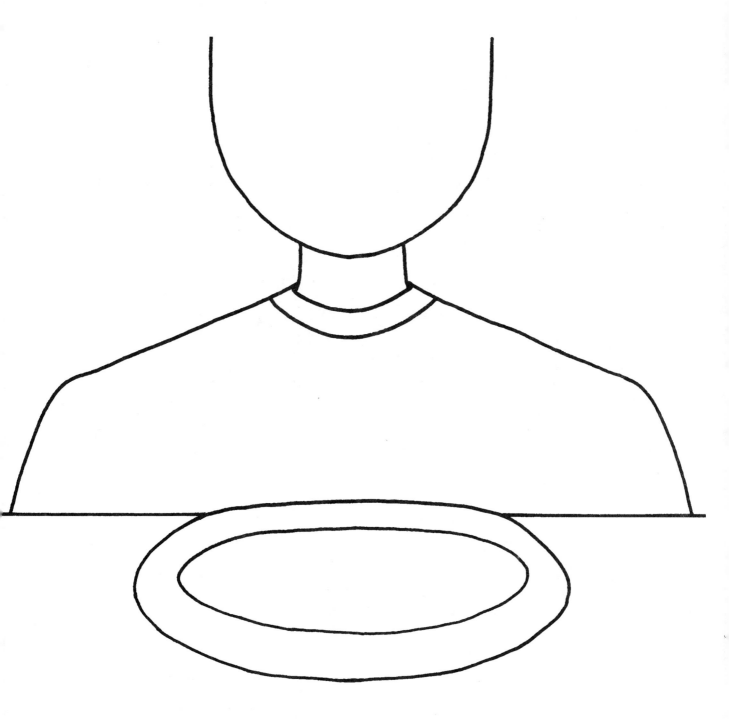

Monday	Stringbeans
Tuesday	Spaghetti
Wednesday	Zooooop
Thursday	Roast Beef

Fresh Fish	Friday
Chicken	Saturday
Ice Cream	Sunday

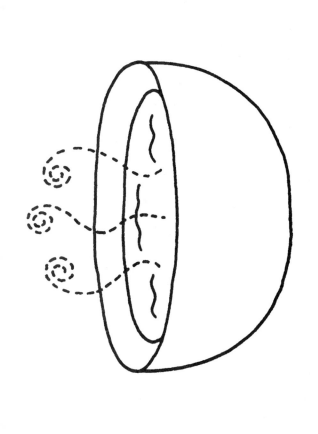

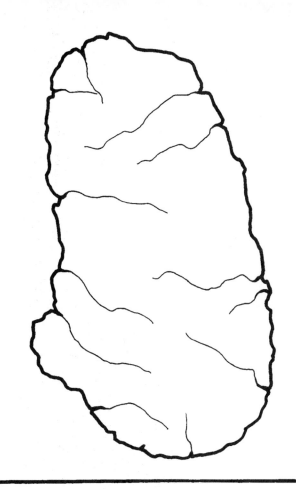

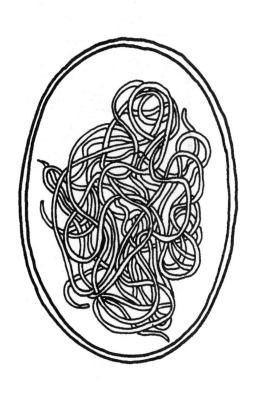

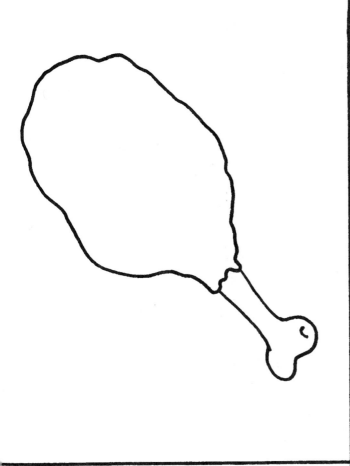

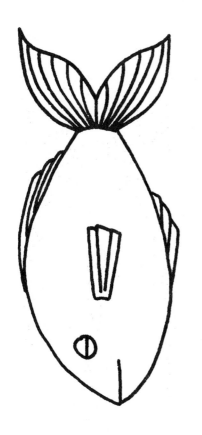

Sam

Hannah

Victoria

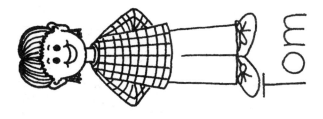

Tom

Victoria

Sam

The Doorbell Rang ①

③

Peter's little brother   Peter   Hannah   Tom   Sam   Victoria

④

Peter's little brother   Peter   Hannah   Tom   Sam   Victoria

cousin   cousin   cousin   cousin   Simon   Joy

45

Like ☺	Don't Like 😖

Sweet	Not Sweet

Grow above ground	Grow below ground

Vegetable	Fruit

TASTING TIME

51

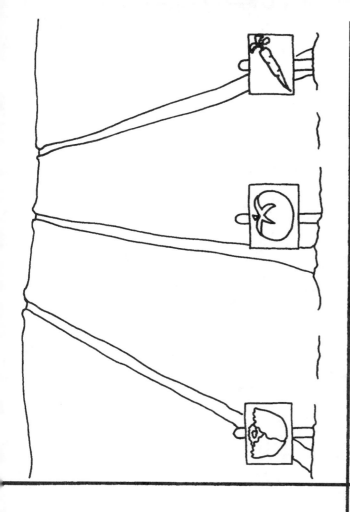

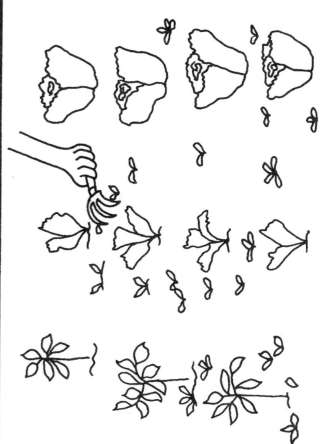

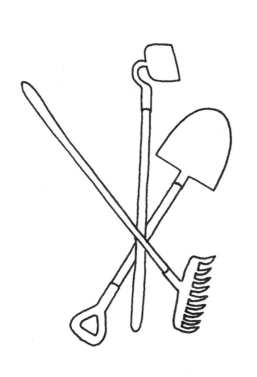

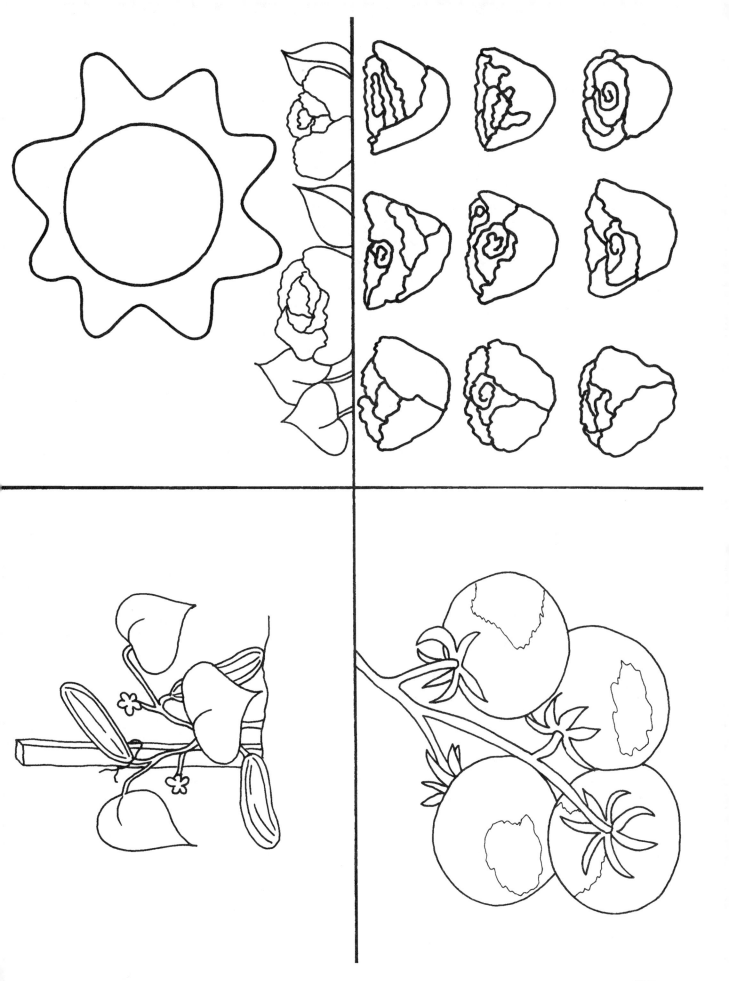

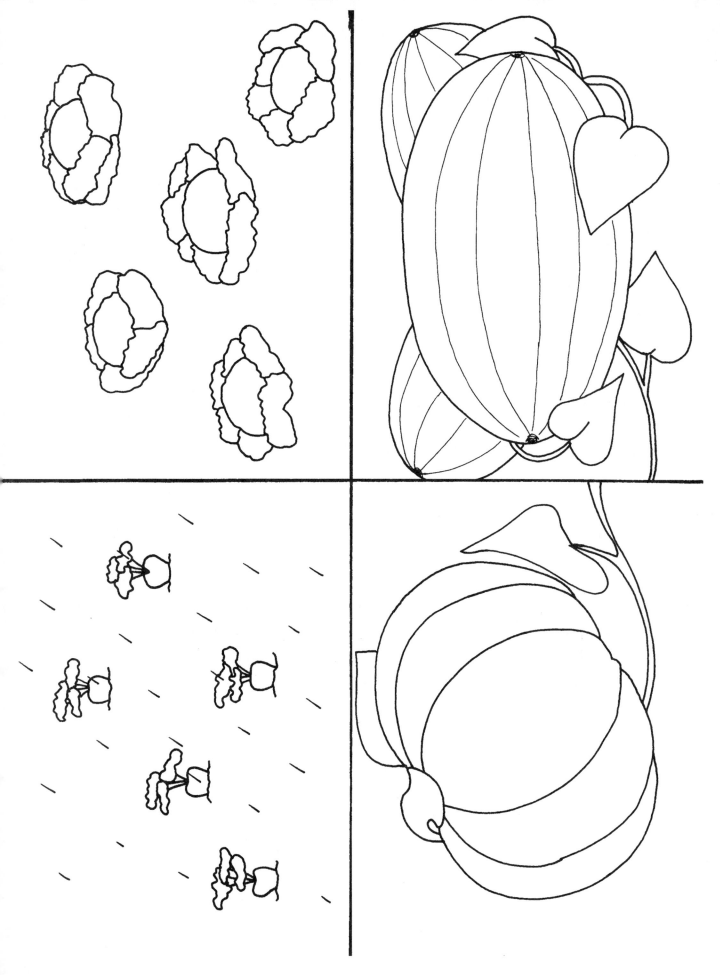

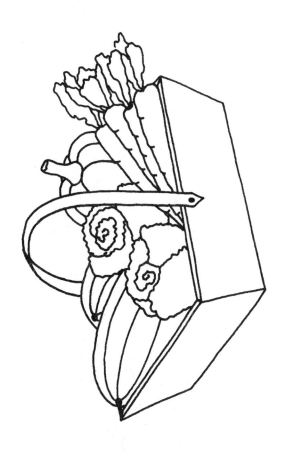

See the _____ grow.
See the _____ grow.
Fruits and veggies in a row,
See the _____ grow.

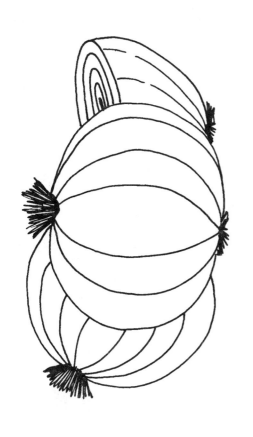

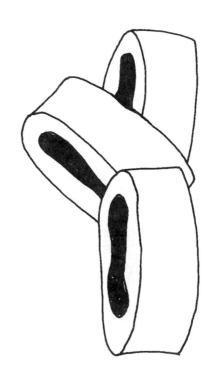

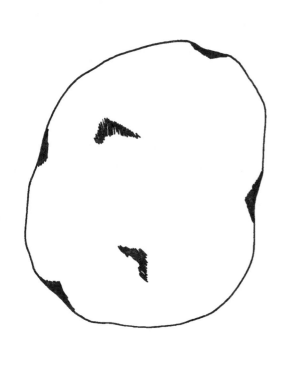

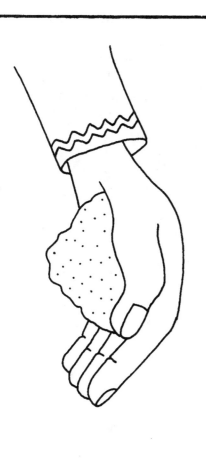

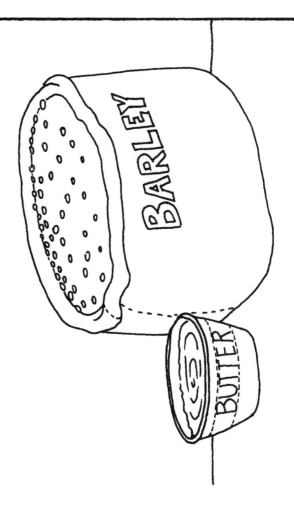

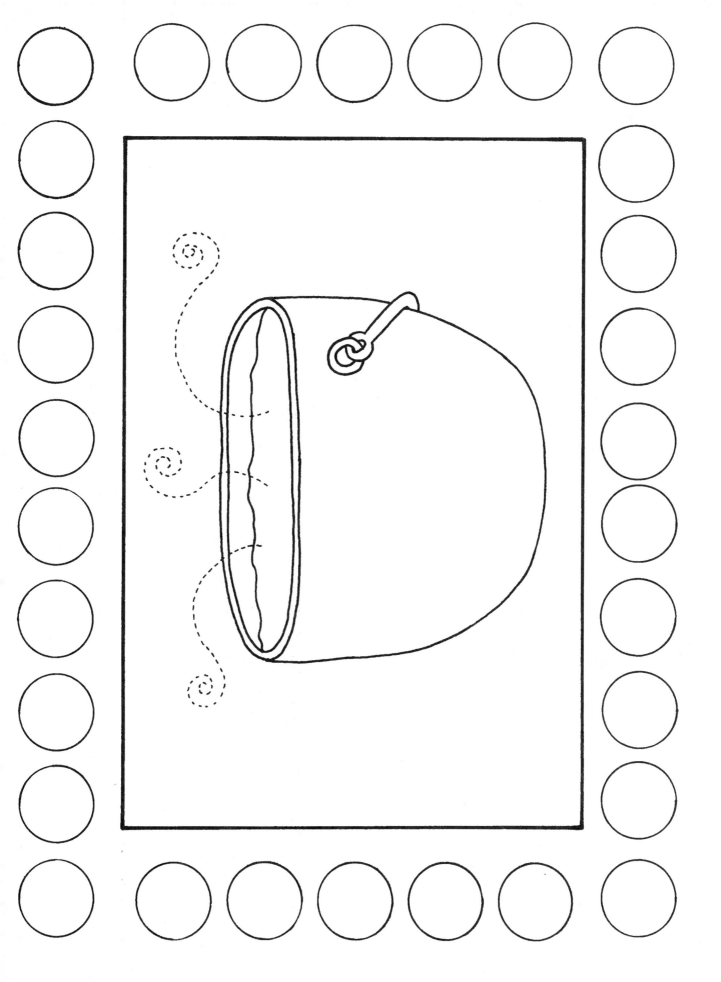

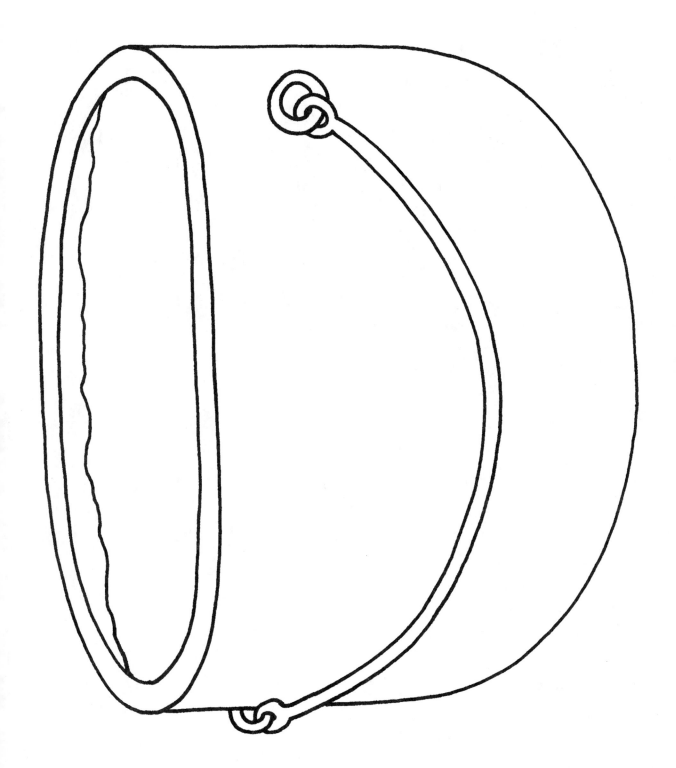

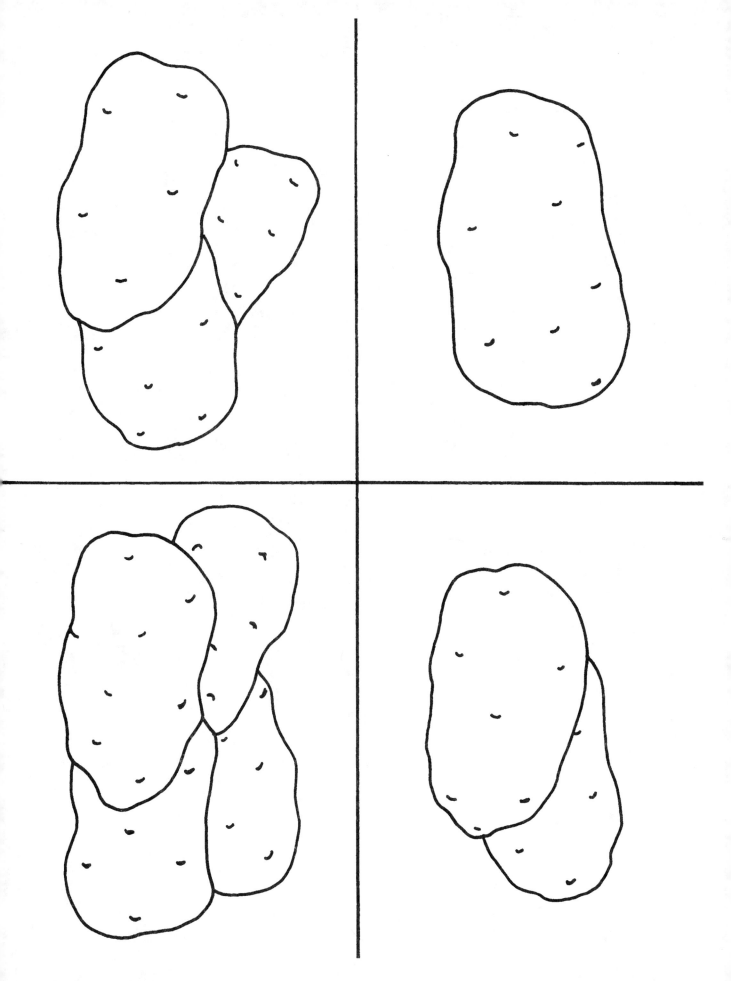

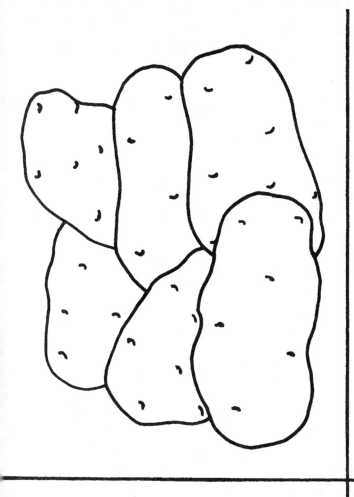

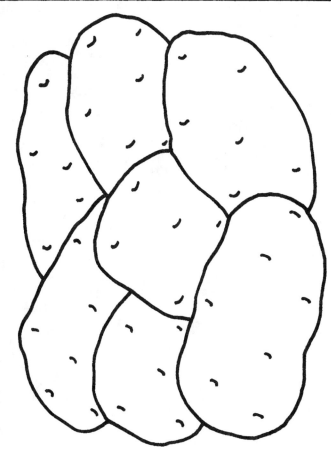

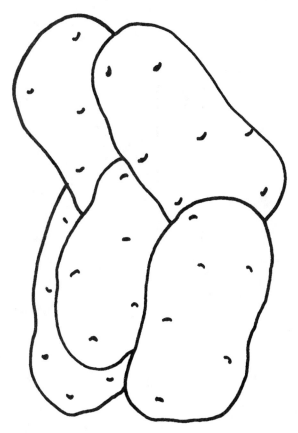

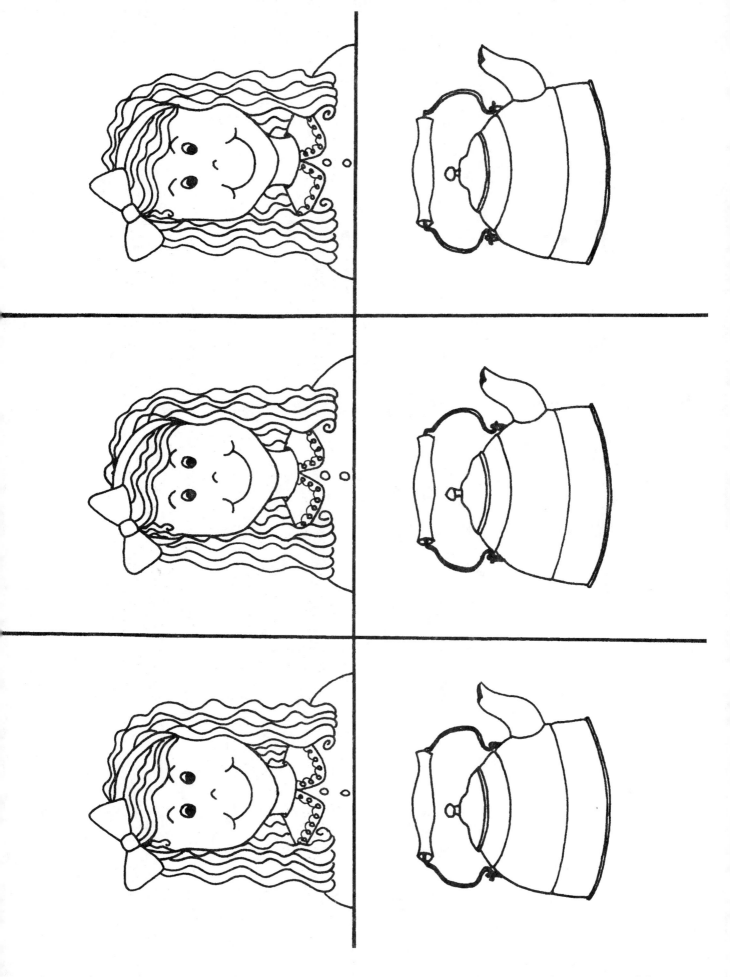

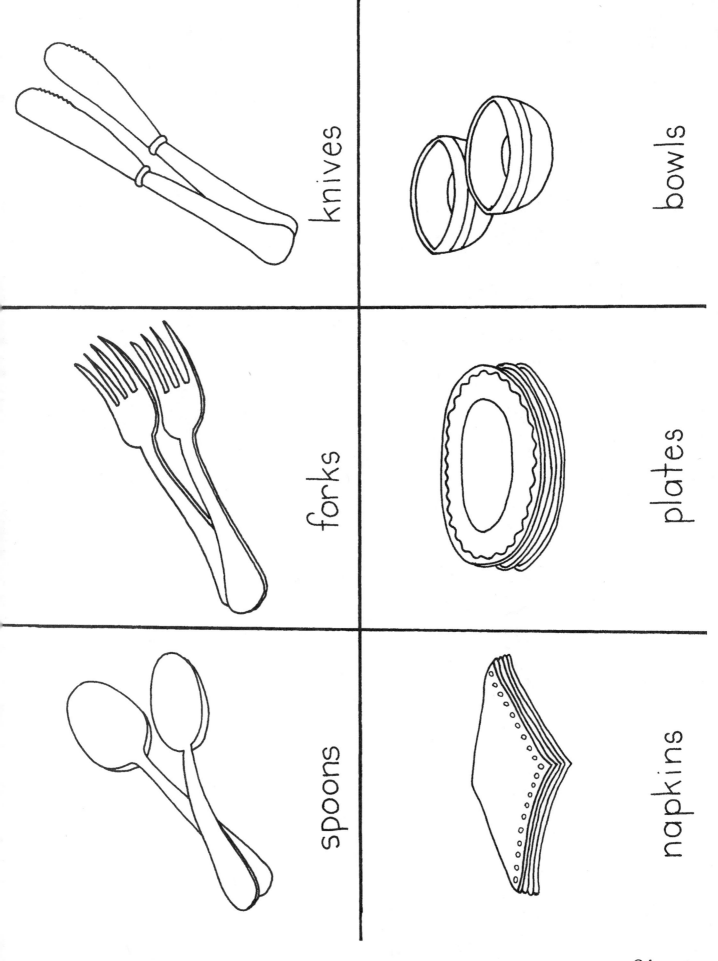

knives

bowls

forks

plates

spoons

napkins

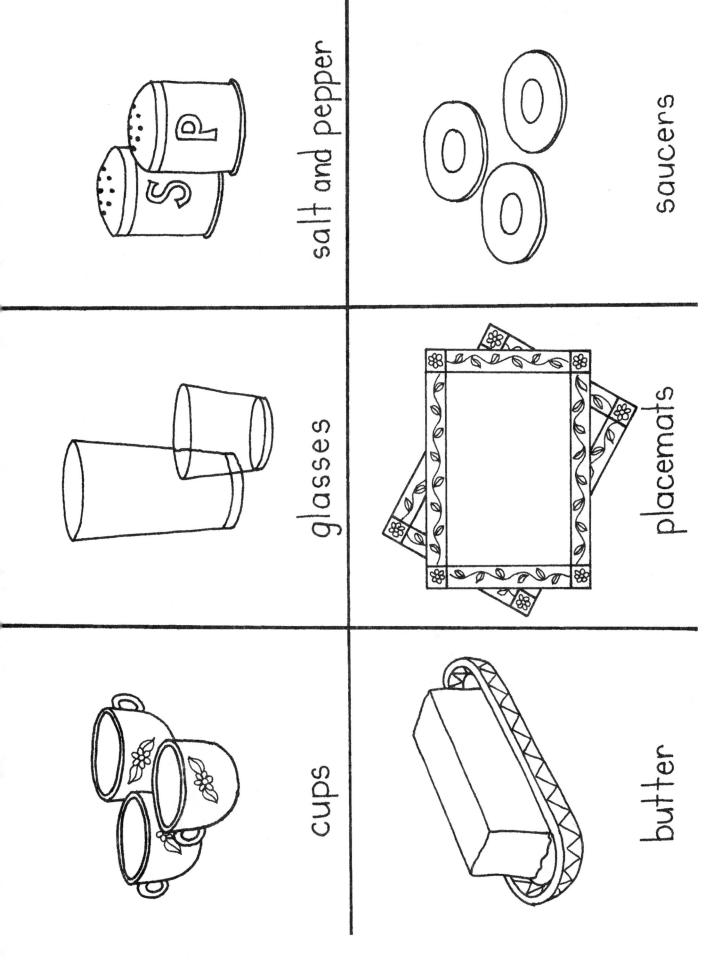

salt and pepper

saucers

glasses

placemats

cups

butter

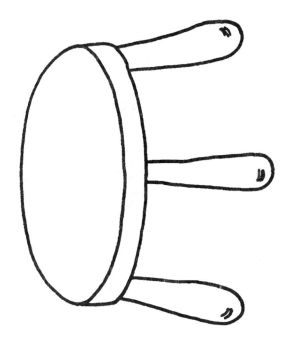

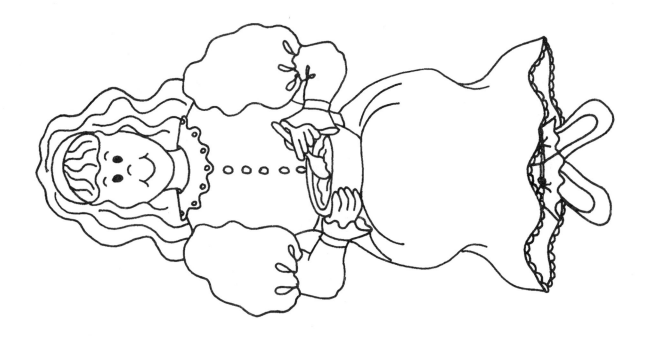

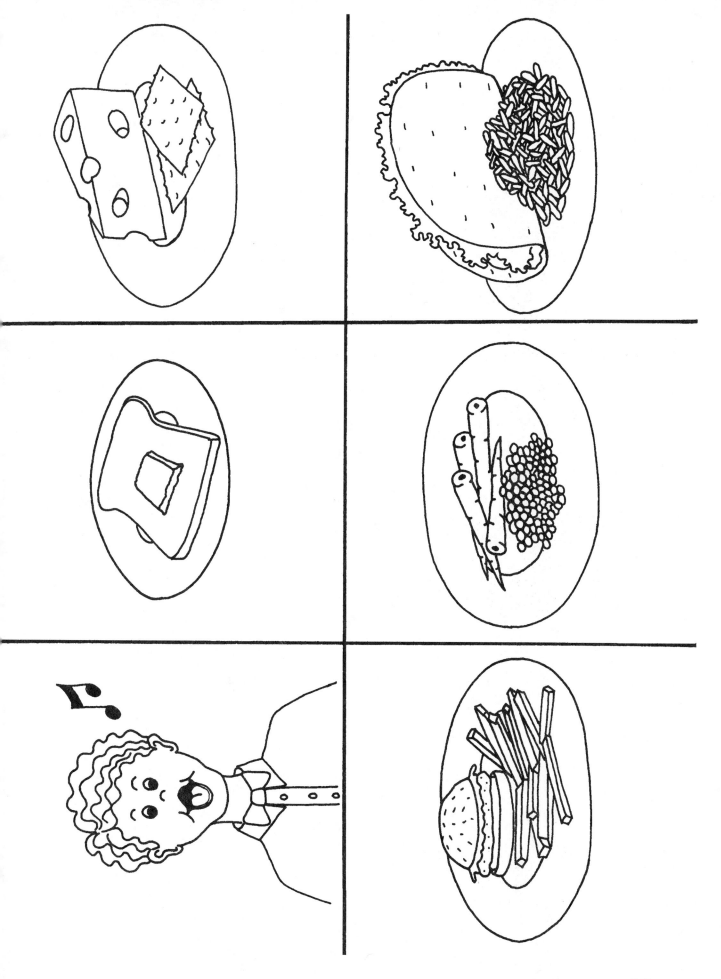

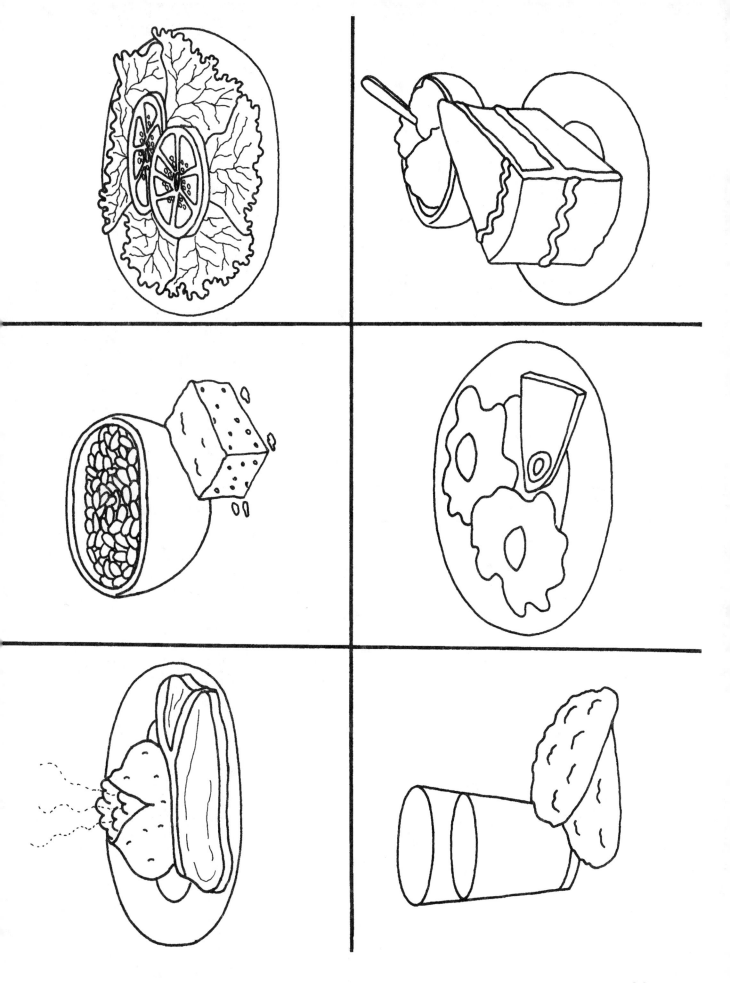

69

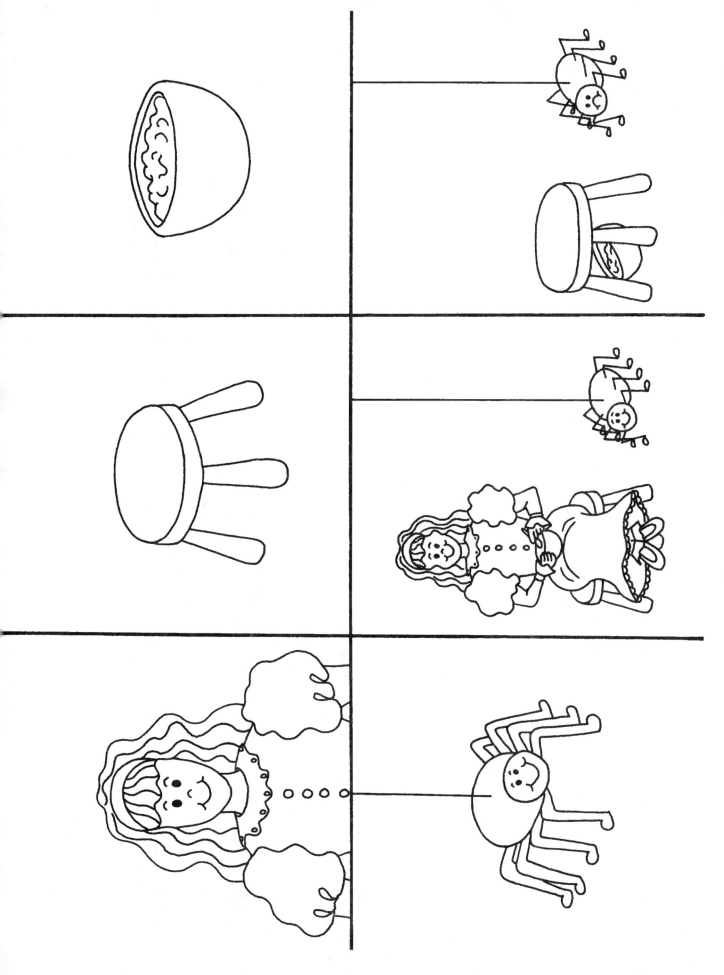

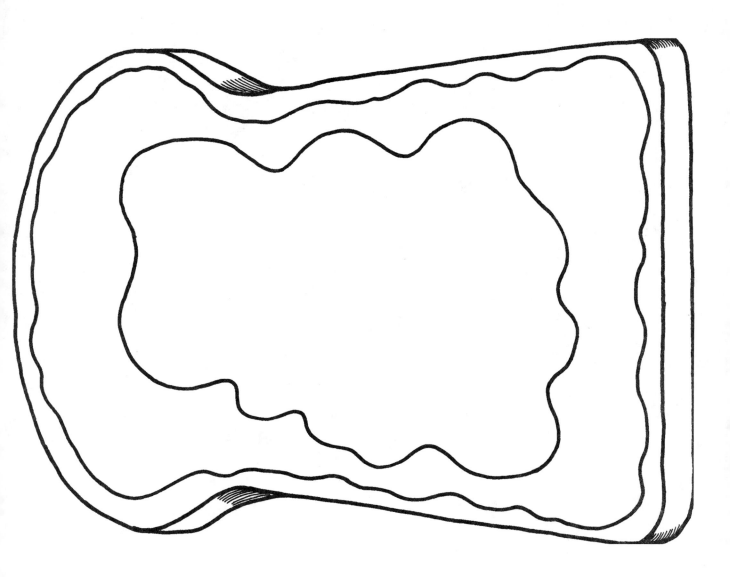

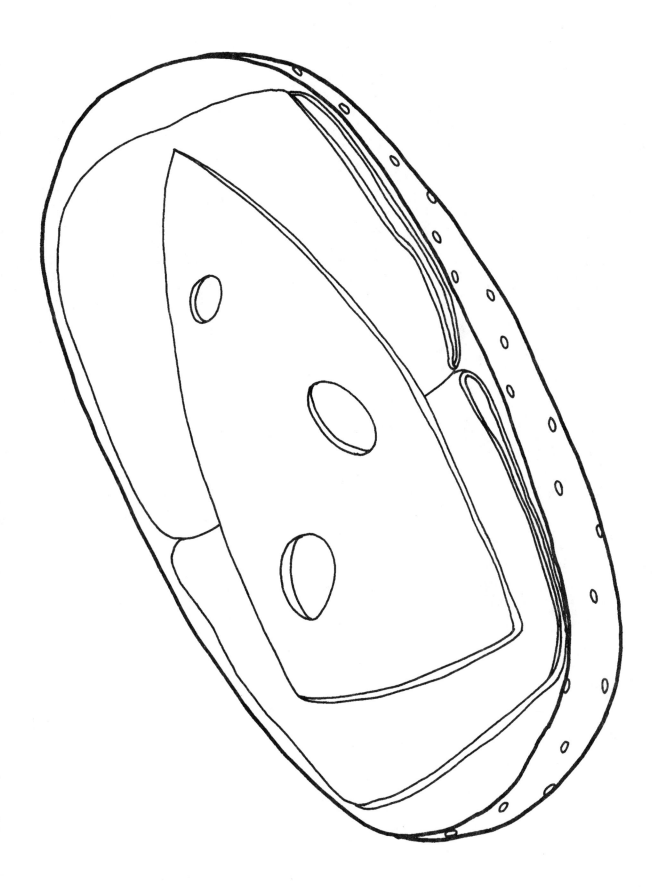

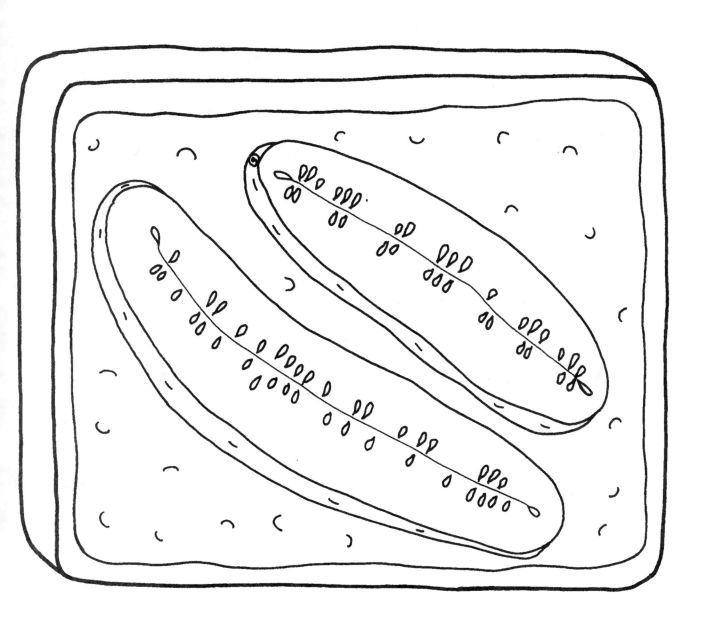

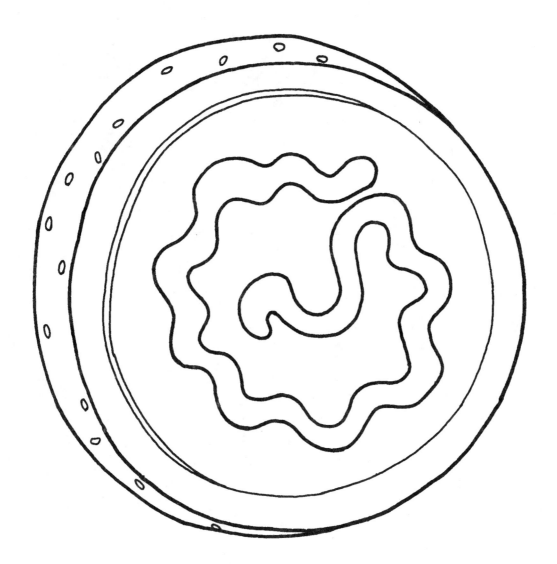

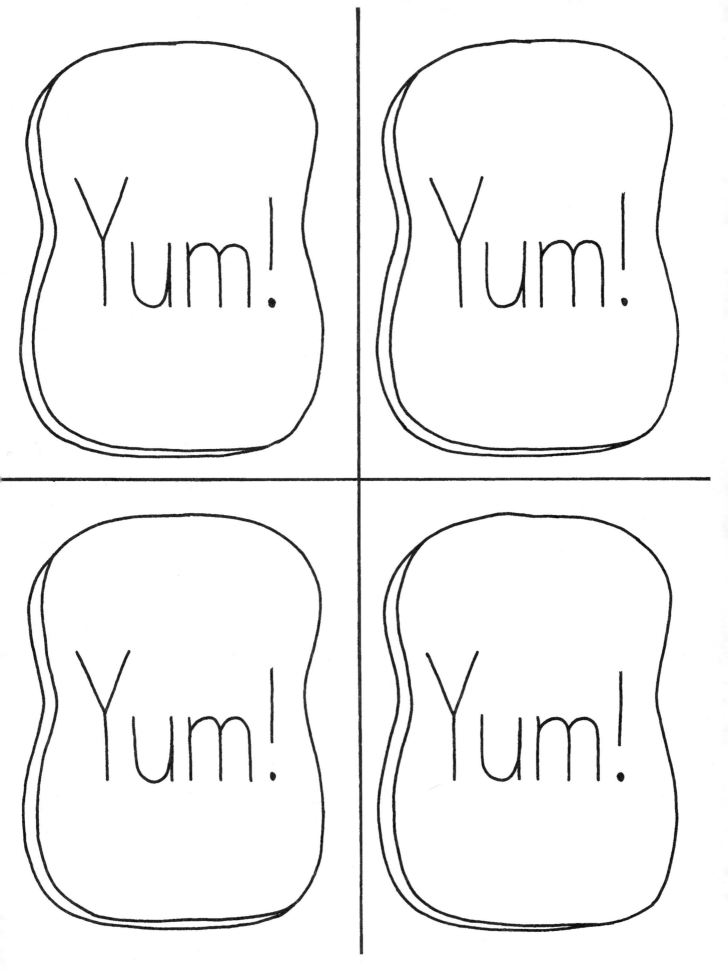

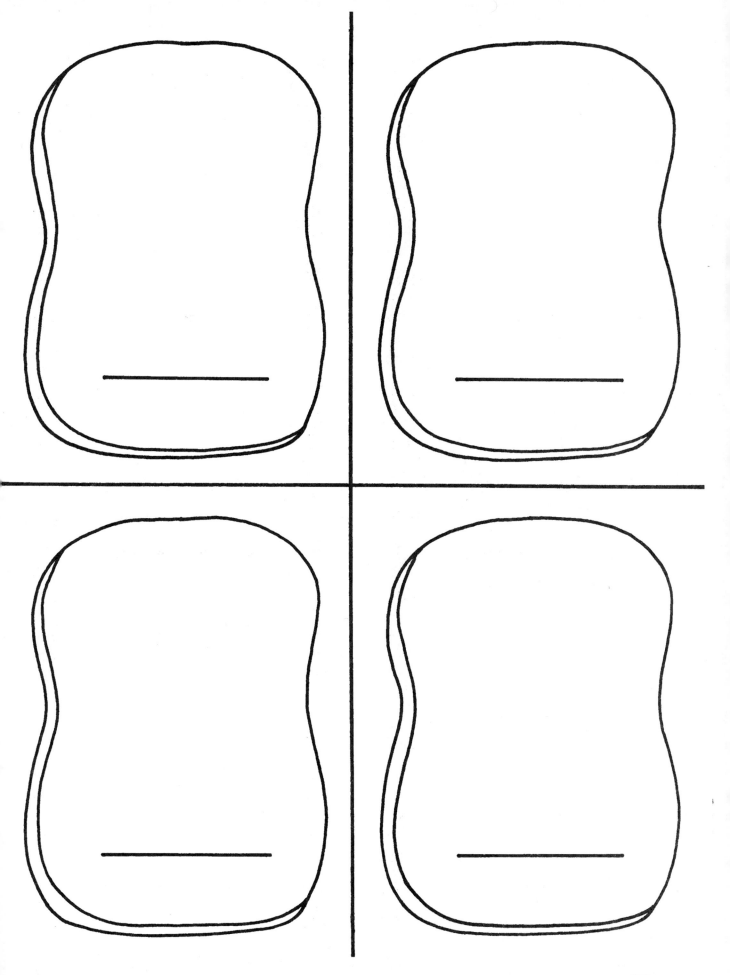

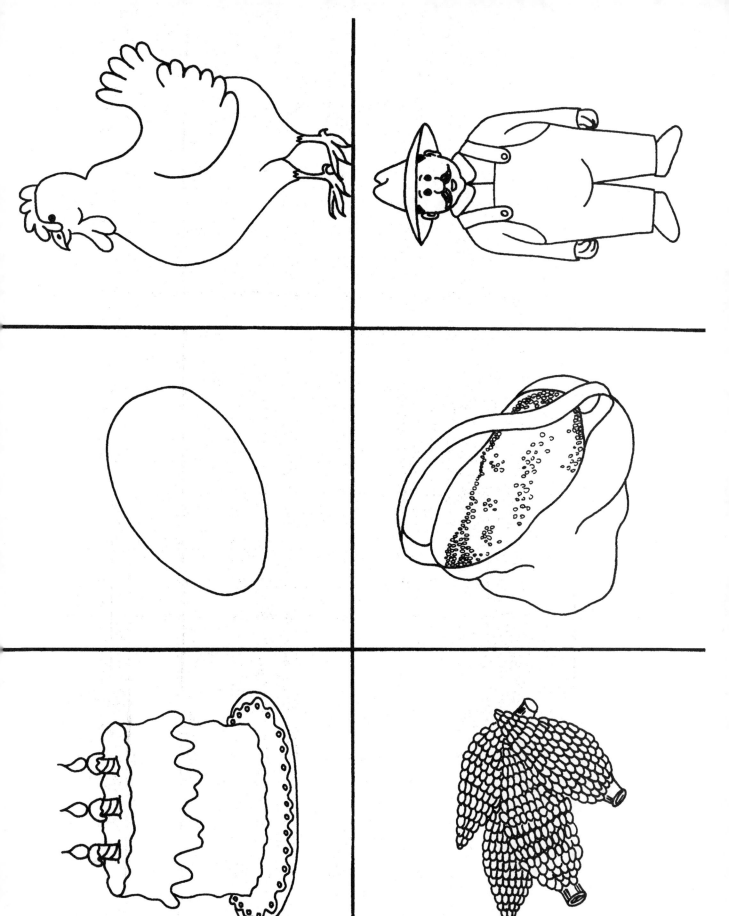

mashed

boiled

baked

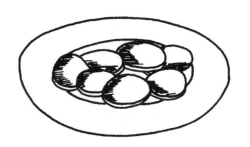
fried

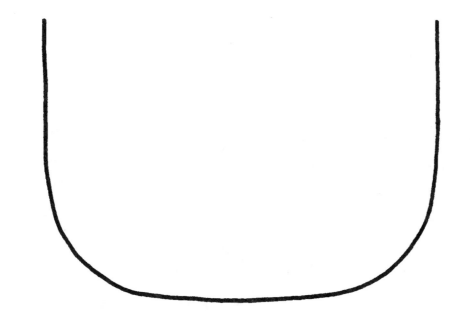

Aikendrum

is for